Hillsborough Entertains

HILLSBOROUGH ENTERTAINS

The Concours d'Elegance Cookbook

Presented by the Concours Cookbook Committee

Foreword by Bonnie Stewart Mickelson

Illustrations by Roy E. Dryer, III

A note on style. We have adopted a few conventions that we hope will make *Hillsborough Entertains* easier to use. Unless otherwise specified, use dried herbs, yellow onions, medium-sized vegetables, and preheat oven to temperature given in recipe instructions.

Editor: Kimberley Peterson
Text and Cover Design: Matrix Productions
Typesetting: Walker Graphics
Printing: Arcata Graphics

Published by the Concours Cookbook Committee
Associated Parents' Groups of Hillsborough, Inc.
300 El Cerrito Avenue
Hillsborough, CA 94010

ISBN 0-9616566-0-3
9 8 7 6 5 4 3 2 1

ACKNOWLEDGMENTS

Thirty years ago, our artist, Roy Dryer, was introduced to fine automobiles at the first Concours d'Elegance. This event, which happened when he was only six, proved to be a major influence in his life. We are grateful to him for portraying in our cookbook so many of the fine automobiles and horseless carriages that have graced the field at the Concours over the years.

We also want to thank Bonnie Stewart Mickelson for her many valuable suggestions and guidance in helping the cookbook to become a reality. Bonnie Mickelson is the well-known editor of the Junior League of Palo Alto's *Private Collections* and *The Overlake School Cookbook.* Her expertise in both compiling and producing our cookbook is deeply appreciated.

CONCOURS COOKBOOK COMMITTEE

Ellen Spiegel
Chairman

Committee Members

Linda Applegarth	Diane Di Costanza	Lynn Kiley	Judy Standridge
Marcia Barkoff	Rosi Fordwood	Susanne Lauridsen	Nattie Trevor
Eileen Benzian	Barbara Frank	Bettie Marx	Becky Witter
Melinda Brann	Jane Green	Diane Matagrano	Linda Zucker
	Bonnie Hepps	Maxine Plotkin	

Sponsored by Willem, Ellen, Fleur, and Edward Spiegel

CONTENTS

FOREWORD

Cooking is more than a necessary task for the consumption of food. It is a way of embodying one's own personality in relationship to those one wishes to please. It is soul-satisfying ... providing succor for our human need to give and to be appreciated. So each cook prides herself on her expertise in presenting attractive and delicious foods. Naturally, this attitude prevails in the formation of a cookbook.

However, creating and publishing a cookbook is no small endeavor. Even the biggest of publishing houses would agree that compiling, writing, editing, and producing a collection of recipes can be a monumental task. Such a project undertaken by a committee of volunteers serving a nonprofit organization can stretch into years of literal blood, sweat, and tears.

Those of you who have survived such travails know that each committee member, justifiably, has his or her own vision of the end product, and deep, deep convictions as to the path that should be taken to realize that vision.

Culminating all the energies and ideas of eager participants into a cookbook of merit requires patience and tolerance, leadership and cooperation, vision and temperance. It is truly remarkable that the Concours Cookbook Committee managed to achieve this in little over eight months ... and they did it well!

As you read through *Hillsborough Entertains,* you cannot help but feel that the Committee wants you, the cook and the host and hostess, to experience just as much fun and pride in cooking for and entertaining those dear to you as each of its members had in creating this delightful book. I can hardly wait to get to the kitchen!

—Bonnie Stewart Mickelson

Hillsborough Entertains

William F. McClenahan

Sponsored by MAERSK LINE Global Transportation

CALIFORNIA GRILL

·ONE·

Shrimp in Foil
Lime-glazed Chicken
Green Chili Rice
Grilled Corn
Sunshine Spinach Salad
Chocolate Delight Cake

·TWO·

Crudités with Spinach Dip
Peppered Swordfish with Cognac
Rice Pilaf
Marinated Cucumbers
Raspberry Bavarian Pie

·OPTIONS·

Butterflied Leg of Lamb
David's Famous Beans
Ratatouille

Shrimp in Foil

Serves: 4   *Effortless from beginning to end.*
Prepare: 25 minutes
Grill: 10-15 minutes

1   pound raw medium-large shrimp, peeled
    and deveined
⅓   cup butter
1   cup fresh mushrooms, thinly sliced
¼   cup finely chopped onion
⅓   cup finely chopped parsley
½   teaspoon salt
½   teaspoon Worcestershire sauce
    dash Tabasco sauce
    minced garlic and freshly ground pepper to
    taste

Cut 4 12″ x 12″ squares of heavy-duty foil. Wash and dry shrimp, divide in equal portions, and place on ½ of each foil square. Melt the butter in a 1-quart saucepan over low heat. Add remaining ingredients and stir for a few seconds. Pour ¼ of the mixture over each portion of shrimp. Fold foil securely over shrimp; the packages will swell up during cooking but will not burst if properly sealed.

Grill over medium coals for 10-15 minutes. When ready to serve, place the foil packages on a warm plate, cut an X in the top of each package, and serve the shrimp and mushrooms in the foil.

Lime-glazed Chicken

Serves: 8   *Tangy, good, and best of all, low in*
Prepare: 15 minutes *calories!*
Marinate: 2 hours
Grill: 45 minutes

2   3½-pound chickens, quartered

Marinade

5   tablespoons soy sauce
    juice of 6 limes
8   thin slices fresh ginger
2   cloves garlic, crushed
1   14½-ounce can chicken broth
½   cup butter, melted

Glaze

4   teaspoons cornstarch
1   cup dry white wine
3   tablespoons finely chopped green onion

Place chicken in a shallow glass dish. Combine marinade ingredients, except butter, and pour over chicken. Cover and let stand at room temperature for about 2 hours.

Strain off the marinade into a measuring cup and add ½ to the melted butter. Use this for basting the chicken as it cooks. Grill or broil chicken until done (20 minutes on each side).

To prepare glaze, 5 minutes before serving dissolve cornstarch in a tablespoon of remaining marinade. In a saucepan, heat rest of marinade with the wine. Bring mixture to a boil; remove from heat. Whisk in the dissolved cornstarch and return to heat. Bring to a boil and cook, whisking constantly, until thickened.

To serve, coat chicken with this glaze and sprinkle with green onion.

Green Chili Rice

Serves: 6-8   *Good with ham, steak, or chicken.*
Prepare: 20 minutes
Bake: 35 minutes

    2   cups sour cream
    1   4-ounce can green chilies, chopped
    3   cups cooked white rice
    ¾   pound jack cheese, sliced
    ½   cup cheddar cheese, grated

Mix sour cream and chilies together. In a buttered, 2-quart casserole, alternate layers of rice, jack cheese, and sour cream/chili mixture. Top with cheddar cheese.

Bake, uncovered, at 350° until bubbly; about 35 minutes.

For a spicier dish, substitute 1 chopped jalapeno pepper for 1 green chili.

Grilled Corn

Serves: 6   *An all-American favorite with extra*
Prepare: 15 minutes   *zest.*
Grill: 15 minutes

    ⅓   cup butter
    2   tablespoons prepared mustard
    2   tablespoons prepared horseradish
    1   teaspoon Worcestershire sauce
    ¼   teaspoon lemon pepper
    6   fresh ears of corn, husks and silk removed

Melt butter and stir in mustard, horseradish, Worcestershire sauce, and lemon pepper. Place each ear of corn on a 12″ x 9″ piece of heavy-duty foil; drizzle butter mixture over corn. Fold edges of foil to seal securely, allowing space for expansion of steam. Grill over medium hot coals, turning occasionally, for 10-15 minutes.

Sunshine Spinach Salad

Serves: 8 *Adds a zing to ordinary spinach*
Prepare: 20 minutes *salad.*

Salad

1	pound fresh spinach leaves, stemmed
3	hard-boiled eggs, diced
6-8	slices bacon, cooked crisp and crumbled
2	cups fresh bean sprouts
1	8-ounce can water chestnuts, sliced

Dressing

1	cup oil
⅔	cup sugar
	salt to taste
1	onion, grated
¼	cup vinegar
⅓	cup catsup
1	tablespoon Worcestershire sauce

Tear spinach into bite-size pieces in a salad bowl. Add remaining salad ingredients.

Mix dressing ingredients together. Pour over salad and toss.

Chocolate Delight Cake

Serves: 20 *A great favorite and so easy to make.*
Prepare: 30 minutes
Bake: 30 minutes

Cake

1	cup butter
1	cup water
4	heaping tablespoons cocoa
2	cups sugar
2	cups flour
½	teaspoon salt
2	eggs
1	cup sour cream
1	teaspoon baking soda

Icing

½	cup butter
4	heaping tablespoons cocoa
1	pound powdered sugar
6	tablespoons milk
1	teaspoon vanilla
	slivered almonds (optional)

Melt butter with water and cocoa in a large saucepan over low heat. Add sugar, flour, and salt. Remove from heat and beat until smooth. Add eggs, sour cream, and baking soda, beating well. Pour into a greased 10" x 15" pan and bake at 375° for 30 minutes. Allow to cool before icing.

To make icing, combine all ingredients in medium saucepan. and heat until butter is melted, stirring constantly. Remove from heat and beat until smooth. Pour over cake and sprinkle with slivered almonds.

Crudités with Spinach Dip

Serves: 8
Prepare: 25 minutes
Chill: overnight,
*   1 hour*

This dip should be prepared 24 hours in advance so the flavors can blend nicely.

1   package frozen chopped spinach (or 2 cups fresh spinach, finely chopped)
1   cup sour cream
½   cup mayonnaise
½   cup minced fresh parsley
½   cup minced green onions (whites only)
½   teaspoon Beau Monde seasoning
½   teaspoon dried dill weed
    salt and pepper to taste
    cucumber, zucchini, carrots, celery, radishes, cauliflower, and snow peas, all cut into bite-size pieces
    endive
1   large head red cabbage, hollowed out*

Cook frozen spinach according to package directions. If using fresh spinach, steam until limp, then drain and press in sieve to dry thoroughly.

In a bowl, combine sour cream, mayonnaise, parsley, scallions, seasonings, and spinach. Cover and refrigerate overnight.

Prepare vegetables and chill in refrigerator for 1 hour. Serve dip in a hollowed-out red cabbage on a tray surrounded by vegetables and garnished with endive.

Peppered Swordfish with Cognac

Serves: 6
Prepare: 15 minutes
Grill: 10 minutes

Any firm-fleshed fish suits this simply delicious recipe.

6   1"-thick swordfish steaks
    salt (optional)
2   tablespoons whole peppercorns, crushed
¼   cup cognac or brandy
    softened butter mixed with minced fresh herbs to taste (basil and chopped chives are good)

Season fish with salt, if desired. Press pepper into both sides of steaks, using the heel of your hand. Grill over hot coals, 5 minutes to a side. Warm cognac in a small pan on the grill while fish cooks.

Transfer fish to a shallow serving platter, pour warmed cognac over it, and flame. Top with dollop of herbed butter.

*To hollow out cabbage, cut a deep X into its top, being careful not to cut through the bottom. Cut a large circle around the X, close to the outside shell. Remove interior to form a deep bowl.

Rice Pilaf

Serves: 8
Prepare: 30 minutes
Cook: 30-40 minutes

An interesting and prettily served pilaf... wonderful with lamb.

Rice

8   cups chicken or beef broth
1½   cups long-grain white rice
4   tablespoons butter

Fruit-almond Mixture

3   tablespoons butter
½   cup blanched whole almonds
¾   cup dried apricots
¾   cup pitted dried prunes
¾   cup seedless raisins or currants
1   tablespoon sugar (or to taste)
¼   teaspoon cinnamon

Bring broth to boil in a large pot over high heat. Slowly add rice, making sure broth continues to boil. Boil vigorously, uncovered, for 10 minutes, stirring carefully 2 or 3 times. Drain well, rinse with lukewarm water, and drain again. Set aside.

Melt 2 tablespoons of butter in large heavy saucepan. Add several tablespoons of rice and mix gently with the butter, spreading evenly over bottom of pan (do not break or mash rice). Add remaining rice to pan and spread evenly over first layer.

Melt 2 tablespoons butter and drizzle over rice. Place kitchen towel over top of pan. Cover pan with lid and pull corners of towel up over lid and pin together (towel will absorb steam). Simmer over low heat for 30-40 minutes.

To make fruit-almond mixture, melt ½ tablespoon butter in large skillet over low heat. Add almonds and sauté until golden. Remove nuts from pan, add remaining butter, and melt over medium heat. Add apricots, prunes, and raisins (or currants), stirring to coat evenly with butter. Sprinkle with sugar and cook gently, stirring frequently until thoroughly heated. Mix in almonds and cinnamon.

To serve, mound pilaf on heated platter and top with fruit mixture.

Marinated Cucumbers

Serves: 8
Prepare: 1 hour
Marinate: 3 hours

A refreshing accompaniment to the rice pilaf.

Cucumbers

3 large cucumbers
  salt
¾ cup cider vinegar
¼ cup sugar
4 green onions, finely chopped
¼ cup chopped parsley

Sauce

1 cup sour cream
1 tablespoon sugar
1 teaspoon dry mustard
2 tablespoons cider vinegar
1 teaspoon salt

Peel cucumbers, cut in half lengthwise, seed, and slice very thin. Sprinkle lightly with salt and let stand for an hour, then drain.

Combine vinegar, sugar, parsley, and green onions. Marinate cucumbers in this mixture for 2-3 hours, then drain. Combine sauce ingredients and toss cucumbers gently with sauce.

Raspberry Bavarian Pie

Serves: 10-12
Prepare: 45 minutes
Bake: 12 minutes
Freeze: 8 hours

Beautiful!

Pastry

⅓ cup butter
2½ tablespoons sugar
⅓ teaspoon salt
1 egg yolk
1 cup flour
½ cup finely chopped almonds

Filling

1 10-ounce package frozen raspberries, partially thawed and drained
2 egg whites
1 cup sugar
1 tablespoon lemon juice
¼ teaspoon vanilla
¼ teaspoon almond extract
¼ teaspoon salt
1 cup heavy cream

Cream butter, sugar, and salt until fluffy. Add egg yolk, beating in thoroughly. Mix in flour and almonds. Press into buttered 10″ pie pan and bake at 400° for 12 minutes. Cool.

Place ingredients for filling, except cream, in large bowl of electric mixer. Beat about 15 minutes, until mixture thickens and expands in volume. Whip cream and fold into raspberry mixture. Fill pastry with this mixture and freeze at least 8 hours. Thaw for ½ hour before serving.

Butterflied Leg of Lamb

Serves: 8
Prepare: 20 minutes
Marinate: 6-8 hours
Grill: 30-45 minutes

This is an easy, prepare-ahead dish that everyone will like, even those who don't care for lamb.

1   cup dry red wine
¾   cup beef stock
3   tablespoons orange marmalade
2   tablespoons red wine vinegar
1   tablespoon minced dried onion
1   clove garlic, crushed
1   tablespoon marjoram
1   tablespoon rosemary
1   large bay leaf, crumbled
1   teaspoon seasoned salt
¼   teaspoon ginger
1   6-7 pound leg of lamb, boned and butterflied

In a 2-quart saucepan, combine all ingredients except lamb and simmer, uncovered, for 20 minutes.

Place lamb in a shallow roasting pan, fat side down. Pour the hot marinade over the lamb and marinate at room temperature 6-8 hours, turning frequently. (Lamb can also marinate overnight in the refrigerator but must be removed about 3 hours prior to grilling.)

Grill over medium-hot coals for 30-45 minutes. Lamb will be cooked medium. To serve, slice fairly thin on a slight diagonal.

David's Famous Beans

Serves: 12
Soak: overnight
Prepare: 30 minutes
Cook: 2 hours

These spicy beans are great as a side dish or a main course. They taste even better the next day.

2   pounds pinto beans
2   bunches green onions, chopped
1   large white onion, chopped
4   cloves garlic, chopped
3   tablespoons bacon drippings
2   pounds ground pork sausage
½   cup chili powder
1   tablespoon salt
1   10-ounce can mixed tomatoes and green chilies*
1   10-ounce can salsa (mild)
1   pound pepperoni, thinly sliced

Wash pinto beans and soak overnight (at least 12 hours) in enough water to cover.

Sauté onions and garlic in bacon drippings in a large pan over medium heat until onions are soft. Add pork sausage, breaking it up into small pieces. Cook for 20-30 minutes, covered.

*The best brand is Ro-tel Tomatoes and Green Chilies, but you can substitute 1 10-ounce can stewed tomatoes mixed with 1 4-ounce can diced green chilies. If you do substitute, increase chili powder by ¼ cup and add 1 seeded, diced jalapeno pepper.

Drain beans and add to sausage, onions, and garlic. Add enough water to cover. Add chili powder, salt, tomatoes and green chilies, and salsa. Bring to a boil and cook 5 minutes, stirring constantly. Reduce heat to low. When beans stop boiling and begin to simmer, add pepperoni, one slice at a time. Cook until beans are soft, about 1½ hours.

If you wish spicier beans, add another can of tomatoes and green chilies and use hotter salsa.

Ratatouille

Serves: 8   *A very good version of an easy*
Prepare: 30 minutes   *vegetable dish.*
Cook: 20 minutes

1	tablespoon olive oil
2	zucchinis, sliced
1	unpeeled eggplant, diced
2	onions, sliced
½	cucumber, sliced
4	tomatoes, peeled and chopped
3	tablespoons white wine
1	clove garlic, finely chopped
	salt and pepper to taste

Heat oil in a large saucepan until it smokes. Turn heat down very low, add onions, and sauté for 2-3 minutes. Add zucchini and eggplant, cover pan, and simmer for 5 more minutes.

Add cucumber, tomatoes, wine, salt, and pepper and continue to simmer on low heat, stirring constantly. Be careful not to overcook. When the mixture thickens, serve immediately.

Cerrito Collection

Sponsored by David Krone

HILLSBOROUGH LUNCHEON

·ONE·

Bougainvilleas
Spinach Soufflé Roll
Copper Pennies
Endive Walnut Salad
Almond Cake in Raspberry Sauce

·TWO·

Wine Welcomer
Asparagus Bundles
Baked Seafood Casserole
Oriental Salad
Lemon Charlotte

·OPTIONS·

Salmon Mousse
Papaya Chicken
Summer Pasta Salad
Apple Cinnamon Tart

Bougainvilleas

Serves: any number of guests
Prepare: just before serving

A nice prelude to a summer luncheon.

champagne*
orange juice
cranberry juice
sprigs of mint (optional)

Combine champagne, orange juice, and cranberry juice in equal portions. (Let the number of guests determine the quantity, using ½ cup of each ingredient per guest.) Pour over ice cubes and serve garnished with mint sprigs.

*For a non-alcoholic punch, Diet 7-Up is a good substitute.

Spinach Soufflé Roll

Serves: 8-10
Prepare: 30 minutes
Bake: 15 minutes

This makes a lovely luncheon entrée or a first course for an elegant dinner.

Soufflé
⅓   cup butter
6   tablespoons flour
  dash of cayenne pepper
¾   teaspoon salt
1¼   cups milk
½   cup freshly grated Parmesan cheese
½   cup grated sharp cheddar cheese
7   eggs, separated, room temperature
¼   teaspoon cream of tartar

Spinach Filling
2   10-ounce packages frozen chopped spinach
3   tablespoons butter
¼   cup finely chopped onion
1   cup chopped mushrooms
¼   teaspoon salt
¼   cup grated sharp cheddar cheese
½   cup sour cream
8   thin slices sharp cheddar cheese

Line a 10½" x 15" greased baking dish with a buttered sheet of baker's parchment. Melt butter in a saucepan. Whisk in flour, cayenne, and ½ teaspoon salt and stir until smooth. Gradually add milk and bring to boil over medium heat, stirring constantly. Reduce heat and continue to stir until thick.

Add cheeses and stir until well blended. Whisk egg yolks and add to cheese mixture. Beat egg whites until stiff, adding cream of tartar and remaining ¼ teaspoon salt while beating. Fold into the cheese mixture. Turn into pan and bake at 350° for 15 minutes or until puffed but firm to the fingertip.

While soufflé bakes, cook spinach according to package directions, and press into sieve to dry. Sauté onion and mushrooms in 1 tablespoon butter, drain excess fluid, and combine with spinach, salt, grated cheese, and sour cream. Mix well and remove from heat.

Loosen baked soufflé and invert on a fresh sheet of baker's parchment that has been lightly sprinkled with Parmesan cheese. Peel off used parchment and spread surface of soufflé with spinach filling. From long side, roll up jelly-roll fashion and place seam-side down on greased cookie sheet. Arrange cheese slices over top and broil until cheese begins to melt. Slice and serve in 1″ thick rounds.

Copper Pennies

Serves: 10-12
Prepare: 20 minutes
Marinate: 24 hours

This unusual variation on carrots is sure to please your guests.

2	pounds carrots
1	bell pepper, finely chopped
1	onion, grated
½	cup fresh lemon juice
½	cup oil
1	teaspoon Worcestershire sauce
1	teaspoon Dijon mustard
½	teaspoon salt
1	10¾-ounce can tomato soup

Cut carrots into thin rounds and steam until tender. While carrots are steaming, prepare bell pepper and onion, combine them with remaining ingredients, and stir well.

Submerge cooked carrots in ice water to stop cooking process. (Carrots should be *al dente*; be careful not to overcook.)

Add drained, cooled carrots to sauce and marinate for 24 hours before serving. Serve chilled.

Endive Walnut Salad

Serves: 6 　　*Different, easy, refreshing.*
Prepare: 10 minutes

½　cup whole walnuts
1　head endive, torn into bite-size pieces
1　11-ounce can mandarin oranges, drained
½　small red onion, thinly sliced

Toast walnuts on a cookie sheet in oven at 350° for 5 minutes. Toss remaining ingredients with your favorite vinaigrette (such as olive oil and raspberry vinegar) and top with walnuts.

Almond Cake in Raspberry Sauce

Serves: 8-10　　*Serve with freshly ground, richly*
Prepare: 20 minutes　*brewed coffee!*
Bake: 1 hour

Cake

8　ounces almond paste
8　tablespoons butter, softened
¾　cup sugar
¼　teaspoon almond extract
1　tablespoon Amaretto liqueur
3　eggs
¼　cup flour
½　teaspoon baking powder

Raspberry Purée

1　10-ounce package frozen raspberries
2　tablespoons sugar
1　tablespoon Amaretto liqueur

Cream almond paste and butter until smooth, then add, beating well, sugar, almond extract, and Amaretto liqueur. Add eggs one at a time, beating well after each is added. Add flour and baking powder, mix well, and pour into buttered, floured, and sugared 8″ springform pan. Bake at 350° for 1 hour. Cool before removing from pan.

While cake bakes, purée thawed raspberries, sugar, and liqueur in a blender. When cake is cool, cover the bottom of a rimmed serving plate with purée mixture and center the cake on top. Sift powdered sugar over top of the cake before serving.

This can be made a day ahead and assembled before serving.

Wine Welcomer

Serves: 10-12   *A very pretty punch.*
Prepare: 5 minutes

2   cups orange juice
1   6-ounce can lemonade concentrate
1   cup orange liqueur
1   liter white wine
1   28-ounce bottle club soda
      orange slices and mint sprigs (optional)

Combine orange juice, lemonade concentrate, liqueur, and wine in punch bowl. Add club soda. Gently stir. Float an ice ring in punch and garnish with orange slices and mint sprigs, if desired.

Asparagus Bundles

Serves: 8-10   *There couldn't be a prettier way to*
Prepare: 30 minutes   *present a vegetable!*
Soak: 4 hours
Cook: 2-4 minutes

1   9" carrot, peeled
1   cup homemade mayonnaise (see page 24)
¾   teaspoon curry powder
1   pound pencil-thin asparagus

To make ribbons, slice carrot into long, thin strips, about ⅛" thick. Soak in salt water for at least 4 hours or overnight. This will make the carrot strips pliable enough to easily tie up the bundles.

To make sauce, add curry powder to homemade mayonnaise and blend well. Set aside.

Blanch asparagus in boiling water for 2-4 minutes or until tender, then plunge into ice-cold water to stop cooking. Drain and tie up bundles of 4-5 asparagus each with carrot ribbons.

The asparagus bundles may be chilled or served at room temperature. Serve with sauce on the side, or you may wish to use the Mustard Dressing from our Moonlight Supper menu (see page 42).

Baked Seafood Casserole

Serves: 8   *The perfect luncheon dish.*
Prepare: 20 minutes
Bake: 45 minutes

2	cups shrimp
2	cups crab meat
1	cup chopped celery
1	cup chopped green pepper
½	cup chopped onion
1	cup mayonnaise
1	cup sour cream
1	tablespoon Worcestershire sauce
	salt to taste
½	teaspoon freshly ground pepper
1¼	cups bread crumbs

Combine all ingredients except ¼ cup of the bread crumbs in a buttered shallow baking dish and mix well. Top with remaining bread crumbs.

Bake at 350° for 45 minutes.

May be mixed and chilled overnight before baking.

Oriental Salad

Serves: 6-8   *Excellent as a light appetizer or side*
Prepare: 30 minutes   *salad.*

Salad

8	ounces snow peas
4	ounces mushrooms, sliced
½	cup bean sprouts

Dressing

2	tablespoons white vinegar
⅓	cup oil
1	teaspoon soy sauce
	salt and freshly ground pepper
	pinch of sugar

Combine salad vegetables and chill until ready to serve.

Blend all dressing ingredients well. Just before serving, pour over salad and toss.

Lemon Charlotte

Serves: 8-10
Prepare: 45 minutes
Cook: 10 minutes
Chill: overnight

Light, lemony, and luscious!

1½	envelopes gelatin
1	cup water
8	eggs, separated
1½	cups sugar
	juice of 2 lemons
1	dozen lady fingers
½	pint heavy cream, whipped

Soak gelatin in ½ cup cold water for 5 minutes, then dissolve in ½ cup boiling water and cool.

Beat egg yolks, and blend in ½ cup sugar and lemon juice. Cook over medium-high heat in double boiler, stirring constantly, until mixture forms a custard. Remove custard from heat and combine with cooled gelatin.

Beat egg whites until stiff and fold in remaining sugar. Fold mixture into cooled custard.

Line springform pan with lady fingers, cover with custard, and chill overnight. Serve topped with whipped cream.

Salmon Mousse

Serves: 8
Prepare: 15 minutes
Chill: 3 hours

Serve as an appetizer or as a main dish at a pretty summer luncheon on the patio.

1½	envelopes unflavored gelatin
½	cup water
2	tablespoons lemon juice
1	small slice onion
½	cup mayonnaise
½	teaspoon paprika
2	teaspoons dill
1	1-pound can salmon, drained
1	cup heavy cream

Sprinkle gelatin over ¼ cup cold water. Let stand 5 minutes. Combine gelatin in saucepan with another ¼ cup water and heat until gelatin is completely melted.

Put lemon juice, onion slice, mayonnaise, and gelatin into blender. Blend at high speed for 40 seconds, add paprika, dill, and salmon, and blend at high speed to a purée.

Add ⅓ of the cream and blend for a few seconds, then continue to add cream in thirds. When all cream is used, blend for 40 more seconds. Pour into a 4-cup mold and chill until firm.

Papaya Chicken

Serves: 8   *An ideal salad for large luncheons.*
Prepare: 30 minutes
Roast: 45 minutes
Chill: 30 minutes

1   teaspoon each: salt, freshly ground pepper, Accent, thyme, and basil
4   tablespoons olive oil
4   whole chicken breasts, boned, skinned, and halved
4   papayas, halved and seeded
5   ribs celery, diced
1   cup mayonnaise
1   tablespoon curry powder
2   tablespoons dried onion flakes (optional)
¼   cup sweet mustard
1   teaspoon each: salt and freshly ground pepper
4   tablespoons slivered almonds, toasted (optional)

Combine seasonings and oil, sprinkle over chicken breasts, and roast at 350° for 45 minutes. When cool, cut chicken into cubes.

Combine remaining ingredients (except almonds) and stir into chicken. Spoon mixture into papaya halves and top with slivered almonds. Chill for 30 minutes before serving.

Summer Pasta Salad

Serves: 8   *Delicious!*
Prepare: 45 minutes
Marinate: 2 hours

3   large ripe tomatoes, cut in wedges
1   pound Brie, rind removed, torn into pieces
1   cup fresh basil, cut in strips
4   garlic cloves, finely minced
1   cup plus 1 tablespoon olive oil
½   teaspoon salt
½   teaspoon freshly ground pepper
1   pound fresh pasta, preferably linguine
    freshly grated Parmesan cheese

Combine tomatoes, Brie, basil, garlic, olive oil, ½ teaspoon salt, and pepper in large serving bowl. Prepare at least 2 hours ahead and marinate at room temperature.

Bring 6 quarts salted water to boil and add 1 tablespoon olive oil. Add pasta and boil until tender but still firm.

Drain *immediately* and toss with tomato mixture to ensure that the pasta is hot enough to melt Brie completely. Sprinkle with Parmesan cheese.

Serve at once or when pasta has cooled to room temperature.

Apple Cinnamon Tart

Serves: 8
Prepare: 30 minutes
Bake: 1¼ hours

Can be made a day ahead. Keeps well, if there's any left over!

Tart

1	cup flour
1	cup sugar
4	tablespoons butter, cut into 4 pieces
1	egg
1	teaspoon baking powder
1	teaspoon vanilla
4-6	green apples, peeled, cored, and thinly sliced

Topping

3	tablespoons melted butter
3	tablespoons sugar
1	teaspoon cinnamon
1	egg

In food processor, combine flour, sugar, butter, egg, baking powder, and vanilla. Using the metal blade, pulse on and off until mixture is cornmeal consistency.

Pat into a well-buttered 9″ springform pan. Arrange apples on top. (Use plenty of apples—they will shrink during baking.) Bake at 350° for 45 minutes.

To make topping, combine sugar, cinnamon, egg, and melted butter in food processor. Whirl until smooth and sugar dissolves. Pour over baked apples. Bake another 25-30 minutes at 350° until top is firm.

This is nice served with dollops of sweetened whipped cream or vanilla ice cream.

Dryer '82

CONCOURS TAILGATER

·ONE·

English Mulled Wine
Hot Artichoke Dip
Barbecued Beef Sandwiches
Overnight Layered Salad
Aram Sandwiches
Raspberry Oatmeal Bars

·TWO·

Geri Lane Hot Chocolate
Spinach Dip in French Bread
Garlic Fried Chicken
Woody Wagon Salad
Tuna Baguettes
Chocolate Pie

·OPTIONS·

Bourbon-glazed Ham
Camembert Bread
Magic Cookie Bars

English Mulled Wine

Serves: 15
Prepare: 10 minutes
Stand: overnight
Cook: 10 minutes

The aroma alone will warm your spirits.

2½	cups sugar
1¼	cups water
4	dozen whole cloves
6	sticks cinnamon
3	whole nutmegs, crushed
	peel of 3 lemons
2	oranges, quartered
4	cups lemon juice
4	liters red wine

Combine sugar, water, cloves, cinnamon, nutmeg, lemon peel, and oranges in a large saucepan and boil for 5-10 minutes, until mixture becomes syrupy. Allow to stand overnight.

Strain syrup and add lemon juice (orange juice can be substituted in equal portions for up to half of the lemon juice) and wine. Heat until steaming but do not boil.

To serve, float lemon and orange slices in hot wine.

Hot Artichoke Dip

Yield: 3 cups
Prepare: 10 minutes
Bake: 15 minutes

Garlic makes this incredibly popular appetizer just that much better.

Homemade Mayonnaise

1	egg
1	tablespoon cider vinegar
½	teaspoon dry mustard
¼	teaspoon white pepper
¼	teaspoon salt (optional)
1½	cups light oil

Dip

4	cloves garlic
1	pound canned or fresh artichoke hearts (if using fresh hearts, steam until tender), quartered
1	cup homemade mayonnaise
1	cup freshly grated Parmesan cheese
½	teaspoon salt
	freshly ground pepper to taste

To make mayonnaise, place egg, vinegar, mustard, pepper, and salt in food processor and process 5 seconds, or until well blended. Continue processing and *slowly* add oil in a very thin stream. Mayonnaise will begin to thicken when you have added at least 1 cup of the oil. You can now add the remaining oil at a faster rate.

Process the garlic in a food processor until minced. Add the artichoke hearts and pulse for six seconds, then add the remaining ingredients and process until well blended.

Turn into an ungreased 1-quart casserole and bake at 350° for 15 minutes, or until bubbly.

Serve with toasted rounds of French bread.

Barbecued Beef Sandwiches

Serves: 8-10
Prepare: 45 minutes
Chill: overnight
Bake: 3 hours,
    1 hour

Make this recipe the day before . . . even better, the day before that! You'll wish you had tripled it.

2	tablespoons salad oil
4-5	pounds cross rib or sirloin tip roast
2	large onions, chopped
1	large green pepper, seeded and chopped
2	ribs celery, chopped
2	large cloves garlic, minced
1	cup catsup
1	16-ounce can stewed tomatoes
¼	cup cider vinegar
⅓	cup brown sugar
1	teaspoon chili powder
½	teaspoon each: basil, oregano, ground cinnamon, and salt (if desired)
8-10	onion, kaiser, or seeded rolls, halved

Heat oil in a 6-8 quart Dutch oven over medium-high heat. Add meat and brown on all sides, remove from pan, and set aside.

Reduce heat to medium and add onions, green pepper, celery, and garlic. Sauté until onions are limp. Add catsup, tomatoes, vinegar, brown sugar, and chili powder and mix well. Stir in basil, oregano, cinnamon, and salt. Simmer, uncovered, for about 10 minutes.

Return meat to pan and thoroughly coat with sauce. Cover and bake at 325° for 3 hours or until meat is tender when pierced. Allow to cool slightly, cover loosely, and refrigerate until the next day. (Do not refrigerate in a cast-iron pot).

About two hours before serving, spoon off and discard congealed fat, lift out meat and thinly slice. Return sliced meat to pan, layering it with sauce. Cover and heat at 350° for 55 minutes or until hot and bubbly.

Transport in Dutch oven wrapped in foil and newspaper. Serve within 4 hours, spooning meat and sauce onto rolls.

Overnight Layered Salad

Serves: 8-10
Prepare: 40 minutes

An unusual salad that becomes a hearty entrée by adding shrimp, chicken, or diced ham.

1	head iceberg lettuce, finely shredded
1	bunch green onions, chopped
1	8-ounce can sliced water chestnuts
½	red or green pepper, chopped
3	ribs celery, sliced
1	10-ounce package frozen peas
2	cups mayonnaise
2	teaspoons sugar
½	cup freshly grated Parmesan cheese
1	teaspoon salt
¼	teaspoon garlic powder
¾	pound bacon, cooked crisp and crumbled
3	hard-boiled eggs, chopped
2	tomatoes

Layer all ingredients except tomatoes in the above order in a deep glass bowl. Other vegetables such as mushrooms or bean sprouts may be added or substituted (more delicate vegetables should form the upper layers of the salad). Sour cream may also be substituted in equal portions for the mayonnaise for a softer flavor. Cover and refrigerate overnight.

Before serving, cut tomatoes into wedges and arrange them attractively on the salad. Do not toss before serving; allow guests to serve themselves wedge-like portions that include all layers.

Aram Sandwiches

Serves: 6
Prepare: Soak cracker bread 1 hour; 10 minutes assembly
Chill: 3-4 hours

Easily made ahead of time and stored in foil until served.

1	Armenian cracker bread (14″ diameter)
1	3-ounce package cream cheese, softened
2	tablespoons mayonnaise
1	tablespoon prepared horseradish
½	pound roast beef, *thinly* sliced
1	cup alfalfa sprouts or whole spinach leaves
1-2	tomatoes, *thinly* sliced

Thoroughly wet both sides of the cracker bread by holding it under cold running water. Place between damp towels for about an hour.

Blend cream cheese, mayonnaise, and horseradish together in a small bowl and spread evenly on the softened cracker bread. Layer beef, sprouts or spinach, and tomatoes.

Roll tightly, jelly-roll fashion, and wrap airtight in plastic wrap and then aluminum foil. Refrigerate 3-4 hours or more. To serve, unwrap and slice crosswise into 12 thick slices.

Filling variations:

—spread egg salad over softened cream cheese, then layer with chopped black olives and sprouts.

—mix 2-3 tablespoons of spicy mustard with the cream cheese. Layer thinly sliced turkey, Swiss cheese, onion, and shredded lettuce or sprouts on top of cream cheese.

Raspberry Oatmeal Bars

Yields: 24 bars *Picnics, tailgate parties, after*
Prepare: 10 minutes *school ... a mouth-watering treat.*
Bake: 20-25 minutes

¾   cup unsalted butter, softened
1   cup brown sugar
1½   cups flour
1½   cups uncooked rolled oats
1   teaspoon salt
½   teaspoon baking soda
1   16-ounce jar red raspberry preserves

Cream butter and sugar until light and fluffy. Combine flour, oats, salt, and soda and mix thoroughly with butter-sugar mixture.

Press half of crumb mixture into greased 8″ square baking pan. Spread with preserves. Sprinkle with remaining crumb mixture.

Bake at 400° for 20-25 minutes. When thoroughly cool, cut into bars.

Geri Lane Hot Chocolate

Serves: 12 *Potentially potent!*
Prepare: 20 minutes

10   cups chocolate milk
2   cups light rum
¼   cup Scotch whiskey
½   teaspoon nutmeg

Combine all ingredients in large saucepan and heat over medium, being careful not to scald milk. If you want a less potent drink, increase amount of chocolate milk to taste.

Spinach Dip in French Bread

Yield: 4 cups
Prepare: 30 minutes
Chill: 2-3 hours

Look carefully! This has variations on a popular theme that truly make it a winner.

1 round loaf sourdough French bread
1 baguette, sweet or sourdough
1 package frozen chopped spinach, defrosted
1 cup mayonnaise
½ cup "creole mayo" (mayonnaise with cayenne pepper added to taste)
1 package dried leek soup mix
1 pint sour cream
1 can water chestnuts, chopped

Slice a lid off round loaf and hollow out insides. Cut "insides" and baguette into 1″ cubes.

Combine remaining ingredients and chill for 2-3 hours.

To serve, fill hollow of bread with dip and surround with bread cubes.

Garlic Fried Chicken

Serves: 8
Prepare: 40 minutes
Marinate: overnight
Cook: 30-60 minutes

This tasty chicken becomes a hearty hors d'oeuvre if trimmed wing joints are used.

Marinade

1 cup sour cream
2 cloves garlic, crushed
1 tablespoon lemon juice
1 teaspoon Worcestershire sauce
1½ teaspoons seasoned salt
¼ teaspoon freshly ground pepper
1 whole egg, well beaten

Chicken

1 2½-pound frying chicken, cut into 9 pieces
2 cups all-purpose flour
1 24-ounce bottle cooking oil
garnish (if desired): fresh parsley sprigs, cherry tomatoes

Mix marinade ingredients in medium bowl. Dip individual chicken pieces in marinade to coat. Place coated pieces in large baking dish and spoon on remaining marinade. Cover and refrigerate overnight.

Dredge marinated chicken pieces in flour and fry in medium-hot oil, 1″-2″ deep, until browned and crisp on both sides. Reduce heat to medium-low and fry slowly until tender—approximately 25-30 minutes total. Do not crowd chicken in pan and do not cover. Carefully turn pieces with a slotted spatula, rather than tongs, because the crust is quite fragile.

Woody Wagon Salad

Serves: 6
Prepare: 20-30 minutes

An interesting variation on Cobb Salad.

Salad

½ head butter lettuce, torn into bite-size pieces
2 chicken breasts, cooked, chilled, and diced
2 medium tomatoes, diced
3 hard-boiled eggs, chopped
6 slices bacon, cooked crisp and crumbled
3 ounces Roquefort cheese, crumbled
2 avocados, halved and cut in wedges
1 small head Belgian endive, thinly sliced
1 tablespoon minced chives

Dressing

½ cup red wine vinegar
1 tablespoon lemon juice
1½ teaspoons freshly ground pepper
1 teaspoon salt
½ teaspoon sugar
½ teaspoon dry mustard
1½ teaspoons Worcestershire sauce
1 clove garlic, minced
1½ cups salad oil

Place lettuce in a large salad bowl. Over lettuce arrange chicken, tomatoes, eggs, bacon, endive, avocado, and cheese in wedges. Surround with chives. Toss at the table with dressing.

For dressing, combine ingredients and mix well. This yields approximately 2 cups of dressing; any extra can be stored for future use.

Tuna Baguettes

Serves: 4
Prepare: 30 minutes
Chill: 1-2 hours

These sandwiches become tasty hors d'oeuvres when sliced into ½" thick rounds.

1 6½-ounce can tuna
½ cup diced celery
2-3 tablespoons minced onion
2 tablespoons chopped parsley
¼ teaspoon freshly ground pepper
2 tablespoons each: mayonnaise and Miracle Whip (more or less, to taste)
1 baguette (2½" diameter, sweet)

Drain tuna and flake with fork. Add celery, onion, parsley, and pepper and mix well. Add enough mayonnaise-Miracle Whip to obtain desired consistency.

Cut heels off each end of baguette. Cut into 4 smaller baguettes. With serrated knife, hollow out baguettes, leaving ¼" of bread next to crust and 1" of bread at one end to act as a stopper for the filling.

Butter insides of each hollowed-out baguette (this will prevent bread from getting soggy). Stuff each "tube" with filling. Chill 1-2 hours before serving.

Chocolate Pie

Serves: 6-8   *Luscious!*
Prepare: 20 minutes
Chill: 1 hour

1	cup sugar
4	1-ounce squares unsweetened chocolate, broken into small pieces
⅓	cup flour
¼	teaspoon salt
2¼	cups milk
3	egg yolks, slightly beaten
2½	tablespoons butter
1	teaspoon vanilla
1	10″ pastry shell, baked

Combine sugar, chocolate, flour, and salt in a medium saucepan. Over low heat, slowly stir in milk. Raise heat to medium, stirring constantly until bubbly. Cook one more minute and remove from heat.

Stir a small amount of the hot mixture into beaten egg yolks, then add yolk mixture to chocolate and return to heat. Stir constantly for two minutes.

Remove from heat, add butter and vanilla and stir until well blended. Pour into cooled, baked pastry shell and refrigerate for 1 hour before serving.

Bourbon-glazed Ham

Serves: 12   *A new twist on an old favorite.*
Prepare: 15 minutes
Bake: 2 hours
      20 minutes

Ham

1	12-pound smoked ham, precooked
¾	cup bourbon whiskey
2	cups dark brown sugar
1	tablespoon dry mustard
	whole cloves
2	navel oranges, peeled and sectioned

Relish

1	1-pound bag fresh cranberries
⅓	cup sugar
⅓	cup hot water
½	cup orange marmalade

Place ham fat side up on rack in shallow roasting pan. Bake at 325° in middle of oven, without basting, for 2 hours or until meat thermometer registers between 130° and 140°.

When ham is cool enough to handle, cut away rind with a sharp knife. Score the ham by cutting deeply through the fat until you reach the meat, making cuts ½″ apart, lengthwise and crosswise, in a diamond pattern.

Return ham to rack in pan and raise oven heat to 450°. With a pastry brush, paint ham on all sides with ½ cup of bourbon. Combine remaining bourbon with sugar and mustard and pat firmly into scored ham. Place a whole clove in each diamond of ham. Arrange orange sections on ham with toothpicks. Baste with pan drippings.

Bake ham 15-20 minutes more until sugar has melted to form a shiny glaze.

For relish, combine all ingredients except marmalade in a casserole. Cover and bake 50 minutes in a 300° oven. Stir in marmalade when cool.

Camembert Bread

Serves: 10-12 *Great as an hors d'oeuvre or for a*
Prepare: 20 minutes *tailgater.*
Bake: 40 minutes

1	8-ounce round Camembert cheese
1	cup butter, softened
1	teaspoon garlic powder
4	tablespoons fresh chopped parsley
1	large loaf French bread
	freshly grated Parmesan cheese

Combine Camembert, softened butter, garlic powder, and 3 tablespoons of parsley in food processor until smooth. Slice the bread and spread the processed mixture between all slices and along the top of the loaf. Sprinkle the top with remaining parsley and Parmesan cheese. Wrap loaf in aluminum foil and bake at 350° for 40 minutes.

Magic Cookie Bars

Yields: 24 bars *A nice change from brownies.*
Prepare: 10 minutes
Bake: 25-30 minutes

½	cup butter
1½	cups graham cracker crumbs
1	14-ounce can sweetened condensed milk
1	6-ounce package semisweet chocolate morsels
1	2½-ounce can flaked coconut (1½ cups)
1	cup chopped nuts, cook's choice

In 9" x 13" baking pan, melt butter in oven. Sprinkle crumbs over butter. Mix together and press into pan.

Pour sweetened condensed milk evenly over crumb mixture. Top evenly with remaining ingredients and press down firmly.

Bake at 350° for 25-30 minutes or until lightly browned. Cool before cutting. Store loosely covered at room temperature.

Richard K. Simon Collection

Sponsored by The Otto Marx III family

WEEKEND BRUNCH

· ONE ·

Mimosa
Frosted Cauliflower
Jacque's Bran Muffins
Scalloped Apple with Banana
Eggs Olé
Hazelnut Torte

· TWO ·

Gin Fizzes
Lox and Mini Bagels
Mexican Cornbread Soufflé
Baked Fruit Salad
Sierra Ski Brunch
Toffee Butter Crunch

· OPTIONS ·

Manhattan Clam Chowder
Zucchini Cheese Casserole

Mimosa

Serves: 5-10
Prepare: 10 minutes
Simplicity is truly the essence of good taste!

1½	cups sugar
2⅔	cups orange juice
2	bottles champagne
8	orange slices
8	mint sprigs

Mix sugar, orange juice, and a few mint leaves in blender for 2-3 minutes. Fill glasses ⅓ full of this mixture and add champagne. Garnish with orange slices and mint sprigs.

Frosted Cauliflower

Serves: 10-12
Prepare: 20 minutes
Chill: 2-3 hours
An easy appetizer with a pretty presentation.

1	head cauliflower
¾	cup mayonnaise
1	teaspoon curry powder
	parsley sprigs
1	box salted club crackers

Steam whole head of cauliflower until fork tender, approximately 10-15 minutes. Allow to cool to room temperature.

Combine mayonnaise and curry powder and spread over cauliflower head. Garnish with parsley, surround with salted club crackers, and serve with a small knife to cut into florets.

Jacque's Bran Muffins

Yield: 1½ dozen
Prepare: 30 minutes
Bake: 20 minutes
The batter will keep in the refrigerator up to six weeks!

6	cups bran
2	cups boiling water
1	cup melted shortening
2	cups sugar
4	eggs
1	quart buttermilk
5	cups whole wheat flour
5	teaspoons soda
2	teaspoons salt

Pour the boiling water over 2 cups of bran and set aside.

In a large bowl, combine remaining bran, shortening, sugar, eggs, and buttermilk. Mix flour, soda, and salt separately, then combine with bran/shortening mixture and mix well. Add bran/water mixture and mix thoroughly.

Spoon dough into greased muffin tins and bake for 20 minutes at 400°. (If miniature muffins are desired, use mini muffin tins and bake for only 10 minutes.)

34

Scalloped Apple with Banana

Serves: 8
Prepare: 20 minutes
Bake: 40 minutes

Great for brunch or as a side dish— or it can be served with ice cream for dessert.

2	large, tart apples, sliced
2	bananas, sliced
1	pear, sliced
1	cup currants (more or less, to taste)
3	tablespoons butter
3	tablespoons brown sugar
1	cup orange juice
	cinnamon to taste
	port wine to taste
	grapes, prunes, or other fruits (optional)

Layer half of the apples in bottom of a buttered baking dish; cover with a layer of bananas.

Sprinkle half of currants, orange juice, and brown sugar over fruit and dot with part of the butter.

Layer pears next, followed by remaining apples. Coat with remainder of orange juice, sugar, currants, and port wine. Dot with remaining butter.

Bake at 350° for 40 minutes uncovered. Siphon off any excess liquid with a baster before serving.

Eggs Olé

Serves: 8
Prepare: 20 minutes
Broil: 2 minutes

This egg dish is great even at dinner!

1	dozen eggs, beaten
1	tablespoon freshly ground pepper
1	teaspoon salt
1	bunch green onions, chopped
1	green pepper, chopped
3	banana peppers, chopped
3	tomatoes, chopped
1	2-ounce jar diced pimentos, drained
1	4-ounce can diced green chilies, drained
3½	cups grated Monterey jack cheese
½	cup grated sharp cheddar cheese

Beat eggs with pepper and salt. Add onions, peppers, tomatoes, pimentos, and green chilies. Stir in cheeses and pour into a greased 2-quart baking dish.

Bake at 350° for 20 minutes, then broil for 1-2 minutes or until crisp on top.

Serve with sour cream and mild or hot salsa. (Herdez brand is a great canned salsa, if you can find it.)

Hazelnut Torte

Serves: 10
Prepare: 30 minutes
Bake: 45 minutes

The traditional German version of a marvelous treat.

Torte

7 eggs, separated
1 cup plus 2 tablespoons sugar
1 teaspoon vanilla sugar
1 tablespoon cornstarch
9 ounces hazelnuts

Glaze

1 cup powdered sugar
juice of one lemon

Beat together egg yolks, sugar, vanilla sugar, and cornstarch until smooth. Save a handful of hazelnuts for decoration; grind the rest in a spice mill, blender, or food processor. Beat the egg whites until stiff peaks form. Gently fold the egg whites and nuts into the egg-yolk mixture.

Pour into a well-greased, floured springform pan and bake at 350° for 40-45 minutes.

To make glaze, beat powdered sugar and lemon juice until a smooth paste is formed. Ice top of cooled torte and decorate with reserved hazelnuts.

Gin Fizzes

Serves: 8
Prepare: 15 minutes

Serve in stemmed glasses with a lemon slice perched on each rim.

1½ cups gin or vodka
1 cup lemon juice
½ cup orange juice
⅓ cup sugar
8 whole eggs
2 cups heavy cream
½ teaspoon orange flower water
5 cups cracked ice

Pour all ingredients into a blender and blend well. (This will need to be done in 2 batches.)

Lox and Mini Bagels

Yield: 1½ cups
Prepare: 5 minutes

A fun hors d'oeuvre.

1 8-ounce package cream cheese, softened
¼ pound smoked salmon
¼ onion, chopped
3 tablespoons milk
12 mini bagels, halved

Combine first 4 ingredients in food processor until well blended. Serve in a bowl surrounded by warmed mini bagels.

Mexican Corn Bread Soufflé

Serves: 8
Prepare: 10 minutes
Bake: 45 minutes

A super version of a California favorite.

1 8-ounce can creamed corn
2 eggs, beaten
⅓ cup corn oil
¾ cup milk
1 cup cornmeal
½ teaspoon salt
½ teaspoon baking soda
1 4-ounce can diced green chilies
1½ cups grated sharp cheddar cheese

Combine corn, eggs, oil, and milk. Mix cornmeal, salt, and soda together and add to the milk mixture, blending well. Pour half the batter into a greased 1-quart casserole. Spread the chilies on top and sprinkle with half the cheese. Cover with remaining batter and sprinkle with the remaining cheese. Bake at 375° for 40-45 minutes, until crust is light golden brown.

Baked Fruit Salad

Serves: 12
Prepare: 20 minutes
Bake: 25 minutes

Serve piping hot with a brimming bowl of sour cream.

1 1-pound can each: peach halves, pineapple chunks, pear halves, apricot halves, and pitted cherries
2 tart apples, cored and diced
3 tablespoons lemon juice
½ teaspoon each: ground nutmeg and ground cinnamon
¼ teaspoon ground cloves
¼ cup brown sugar, firmly packed
4 tablespoons butter, cut into chunks
3 bananas, sliced
2 cups seedless grapes
  sour cream

Drain and reserve together liquids from peaches, pineapples, pears, and apricots. Place drained fruit in a 3-quart covered baking dish. Sprinkle apples with lemon juice and combine with drained fruit.

Mix nutmeg, cinnamon, cloves, and brown sugar with 1½ cups of the reserved liquid and pour over fruit. Dot with butter, cover, and bake at 350° for 20 minutes.

Peel and slice bananas, mix with grapes, and add to baked fruit. Return covered to 350° oven for 5 more minutes.

Serve hot with sour cream on the side.

Toffee Butter Crunch

Yield: 2 pounds　　*A dessert candy that kids of all ages*
Prepare: 30 minutes　*will love.*
Chill: 2-3 hours

  2　6-ounce cans roasted, salted almonds
　　(1 coarsely chopped, 1 finely chopped)
 12　1.45-ounce milk chocolate bars
  1　cup butter
1⅓　cups sugar
  1　tablespoon light corn syrup
  3　tablespoons water

Butter a 7½" x 11¾" pan and sprinkle with half of the finely chopped nuts. Cover nuts with 6 chocolate bars.

Melt butter in a large, heavy saucepan. Add sugar, corn syrup, and water. Cook over medium heat, stirring occasionally. Using a candy thermometer, cook to 300°. *Quickly* stir in coarsely chopped nuts and pour over chocolate bars. *Immediately* cover with remaining chocolate bars and sprinkle top with remaining finely chopped nuts. Using waxed paper, press gently so nuts will adhere. Chill. Break into pieces to serve.

Sierra Ski Brunch

Serves: 10　　　*A marvelous version of an ideal*
Prepare: 40 minutes　*brunch or supper entrée.*
Chill: overnight
Bake: 1 hour

  2　tablespoons butter
 12　slices white bread, crusts removed
  ½　pound mushrooms, sliced
  2　cups thinly sliced onions
  ½　cup butter, melted
1½　pounds mild Italian sausage
  ¾　pound cheddar cheese, grated
  5　eggs
2½　cups milk
  3　teaspoons Dijon mustard
  1　teaspoon dry mustard
  1　teaspoon ground nutmeg
  1　teaspoon salt
  ⅛　teaspoon freshly ground pepper
  2　tablespoons finely chopped fresh parsley

Butter bread and set aside. In skillet, brown mushrooms and onions in melted butter. Cook 5-8 minutes or until tender. Cut sausage into bite-size pieces and sauté in separate skillet until done. Set aside.

In a greased 7" x 11" casserole, layer half the bread, mushroom mixture, sausage, and cheese. Repeat layers, ending with the cheese.

Whisk together eggs, milk, mustards, nutmeg, salt, and pepper and pour over casserole. Cover and refrigerate overnight so bread can absorb liquids.

When ready to bake, sprinkle parsley over top and bake uncovered at 350° for 1 hour or until bubbly.

Manhattan Clam Chowder

Serves: 12
Prepare: 60 minutes
Cook: 1 hour,
10 minutes

This chowder tastes even better the next day and freezes well, too!

3	onions, diced
6	carrots, diced
4	ribs celery, diced
2	tablespoons chopped parsley
3	tablespoons reserved bacon fat
1	pound bacon, cooked crisp and crumbled
1	2-pound can whole tomatoes, chopped
4	cans whole baby clams
2	teaspoons thyme
2	bay leaves
3½	cups tomato juice
4	tablespoons lemon juice
	Tabasco to taste
	salt and pepper to taste
3	potatoes, diced

Sauté onions, carrots, celery, and parsley in reserved bacon fat over medium heat until tender. Combine with crumbled bacon and set aside.

Drain tomatoes, reserving liquid, and add chopped tomatoes to vegetable/bacon mixture. Drain clams, adding reserved juice to tomato liquid. Refrigerate clams until needed.

Add enough water to reserved clam/tomato liquid to make 6 cups and combine with thyme, bay leaves, tomato juice, lemon juice, Tabasco, and salt and pepper.

Bring to a boil, add potatoes, cover, and simmer for 55 minutes. Add clams and vegetables and simmer uncovered another 15 minutes.

Zucchini Cheese Casserole

Serves: 6-8
Prepare: 20 minutes
Bake: 30 minutes

A particularly good version ... think of it for barbecue menus, too!

1½	pounds zucchini, diced
1	small onion, chopped
2	tablespoons butter
1	4-ounce can diced green chilies, drained
3	tablespoons flour
	salt and freshly ground pepper to taste
1½	cups grated Monterey jack cheese
1	egg
1	cup small curd cottage cheese
2	tablespoons minced parsley
½	cup freshly grated Parmesan cheese

Sauté zucchini and onion in butter until tender. Mix in chilies, flour, salt, and pepper. Turn into a 1½-quart baking dish. Sprinkle with jack cheese. Mix egg with cottage cheese and parsley and spoon over top. Sprinkle with Parmesan cheese and bake uncovered at 400° for 30 minutes. Allow to cool for a few minutes before serving.

Moonlight Supper

· ONE ·

Marinated Artichokes
Butter Lettuce Salad
Spicy Pork Tenderloin
Spring Rice
Grand Marnier Soufflé

· TWO ·

Spicy Rounds
Lobster Salad
Stuffed Chicken Medallions
Herbed Cherry Tomatoes
Millionaire Pie

· OPTIONS ·

Coronation Chicken
Chocolate Truffle Cake

Marinated Artichokes

Serves: 10
Prepare: 5 minutes
Marinate: 24 hours
Cook: 20 minutes

A nice, light appetizer to precede a substantial entrée.

Artichokes

6	cups water
2	bay leaves, crumbled
½	fresh lemon
1	clove garlic, halved
1	tablespoon olive oil
4	large artichokes
1½	cups small mushrooms, halved

Marinade

1	cup olive oil
	juice of 3 lemons
1	tablespoon Spike
⅓	cup water
1	teaspoon sea salt
¾	teaspoon cream-style horseradish
1	clove garlic, halved

Bring water, bay leaves, lemon, garlic, and oil to a rapid boil in a large pot. Blanch artichokes in boiling water, then place all artichokes in pot and simmer for about 20 minutes. (Do not overcook the artichokes. They are done when the leaves from the center pull out easily.)

For marinade, blend all ingredients except garlic in a blender. Add garlic halves and let marinade sit while artichokes are cooking.

When artichokes are done, drain and remove leaves, cover with marinade, and marinate with halved mushrooms in airtight container in refrigerator for 24 hours. (Turn container from time to time to allow the marinade to thoroughly cover vegetables.)

Serve as an hors d'oeuvre or appetizer in lettuce cups or on beds of watercress, offering toothpicks or small forks.

Butter Lettuce Salad

Serves: 8
Yield: 2 cups dressing
Prepare: 25 minutes

The dressing makes this salad special. Your guests will love it.

Salad

2	eggs, hard-boiled and finely chopped
½	teaspoon paprika
½	teaspoon finely chopped parsley
2	heads butter lettuce

Mustard Dressing

½	cup apple cider vinegar
2	teaspoons Dijon mustard
2	teaspoons dill
¼	teaspoon freshly ground pepper
1	clove garlic, crushed
1⅓	cup oil (equal parts light salad and extra virgin olive oils)

Mix eggs, paprika, and parsley together. Place 2-3 lettuce leaves on each plate. Sprinkle 1½ tablespoons of chopped egg mixture over lettuce.

For dressing, combine all ingredients in blender or food processor and mix until well blended.

Just before serving, drizzle 1 tablespoon of dressing over each salad.

Spicy Pork Tenderloin

Serves: 8   *Great flavors!*
Prepare: 10 minutes
Marinate: 4-24 hours
Roast: 40 minutes

 1   2-pound pork tenderloin roast
 ¼   cup prepared mustard
 ¼   cup honey
 ¼   teaspoon salt
 ¼   teaspoon chili powder

Combine mustard, honey, salt, and chili powder. Coat pork with this mixture, and refrigerate for 4 hours or until next day.

Place marinated pork in foil-lined shallow baking dish and roast at 425° for approximately 40 minutes.

Let pork cool for at least 5 minutes. Slice diagonally.

Spring Rice

Serves: 6   *The green and white contrast is*
Prepare: 10 minutes   *lovely.*
Cook: 25 minutes

 2½   cups water
 2   tablespoons butter
 1   cup white rice
 1   bunch fresh spinach, finely chopped
 ½   cup toasted almonds (optional)

Bring water to boil and add 1 tablespoon of butter and rice. When water boils again, reduce heat to low, cover, and let simmer for 25 minutes.

When rice is done, add chopped spinach and remaining butter and mix thoroughly. Garnish with almonds before serving.

Grand Marnier Soufflé

Serves: 8   *Really worth the effort! Be sure to*
Prepare: 45 minutes   *make a day ahead.*
Chill: overnight

Soufflé

3   eggs, separated
½   cup granulated sugar
2   ounces Grand Marnier
1   cup heavy cream
1   teaspoon vanilla
1   envelope unflavored gelatin
¼   cup cold water

Raspberry Sauce

1   12-ounce package frozen raspberries
1   ounce Grand Marnier
¼   cup powdered sugar

Beat egg yolks in a large bowl. Add granulated sugar and beat until creamy, then add Grand Marnier. In another bowl, beat egg whites until stiff but not dry. In a third bowl, whip cream and vanilla until stiff and set aside. Dissolve gelatin in water.

Stir dissolved gelatin into yolk mixture and mix well. Gently fold in egg whites and whipped cream. Pour into soufflé dish and refrigerate overnight.

Thaw package of raspberries for 10 minutes. Place berries with their juice in blender, add Grand Marnier and powdered sugar, and blend until smooth. Chill before serving.

Spicy Rounds

Serves: 10   *Can be made ahead of time and*
Prepare: 30 minutes   *warmed just before serving.*
Bake: 10 minutes

½   cup chopped ripe olives
4   tablespoons mayonnaise
¾   cup grated cheddar cheese
2   green onions, thinly sliced
¼   tablespoon curry powder
1   sourdough baguette

Mix the first 5 ingredients thoroughly. Thinly slice baguette and spread each slice with cheese mixture.

Arrange rounds on cookie sheet and bake at 400° for 10 minutes. Serve hot.

Lobster Salad

Serves: 8-10   *An elegant first-course salad.*
Prepare: 45 minutes
Chill: overnight

2   fresh lobster tails
1   lemon, halved
2   bay leaves
1   cup chopped celery
¾   cup mayonnaise
⅔   cup chopped Chinese pea pods
   juice of 1 lemon
¾   teaspoon tarragon

Place lobster tails in a pot of boiling water with lemon and bay leaves. Boil uncovered for 12-15 minutes. The meat should be white, not transparent. Be careful not to overcook. When cool, the meat will easily lift out of shell.

Shred cooked lobster and mix well with remaining ingredients. Serve in a lettuce cup, garnished with slices of fresh oranges and grapefruit.

Bay shrimp or crab meat may be substituted for lobster. Sliced water chestnuts and bean sprouts can also be added for an oriental touch.

Stuffed Chicken Medallions

Serves: 8
Prepare: 45 minutes
Roast: 1 hour

A delight to the eye and the palate ... can be prepared ahead of time.

Mushroom Stuffing
½ pound mushrooms, finely chopped
¼ cup chopped almonds
¼ cup finely chopped green onions
¼ cup chopped celery
¼ cup butter
3 tablespoons dry bread crumbs
   dash of salt and freshly ground pepper

Chicken
8 chicken breasts, halved, boned, and skinned
¼ cup butter, melted

Black Raspberry Sauce
½ cup seedless black raspberry jam
⅓ cup honey
2 tablespoons frozen orange juice concentrate
1 teaspoon finely grated orange rind
1 tablespoon lemon juice

To make stuffing, sauté mushrooms, almonds, onions, and celery in ¼ cup butter until most of the moisture is absorbed, then add bread crumbs, salt, and pepper.

Flatten chicken breasts between sheets of waxed paper with a wooden mallet or the side of a cleaver. Place 1 rounded tablespoon of stuffing in center of each chicken breast and roll up. Place seam side down in baking dish. Brush with melted butter. Roast uncovered at 350° for 30 minutes.

While chicken is roasting, combine all ingredients for raspberry sauce and heat over medium heat until melted and well blended.

When chicken has roasted for 30 minutes, coat with raspberry sauce and continue roasting, basting with glaze, until chicken is tender, approximately 30 minutes more. Slice into rounds and serve with extra sauce.

Herbed Cherry Tomatoes

Serves: 8
Prepare: 20 minutes
Bake: 8-10 minutes

Simply elegant.

2   pints cherry tomatoes
½   cup bread crumbs
½   cup freshly grated Parmesan cheese
¼   cup minced fresh chives
¼   cup minced fresh parsley
     salt and freshly ground pepper to taste
¼   cup olive oil

Place tomatoes in a lightly oiled 2-quart baking dish in a single layer.

Combine remaining ingredients (except oil) and sprinkle evenly over tomatoes to cover.

Drizzle oil over all and bake at 500° until tomatoes puff slightly and topping is crusty and golden, about 8-10 minutes.

Millionaire Pie

Serves: 8
Prepare: 40 minutes
Bake: 30 minutes

Rich as rich can be—this is a great dessert to do in quantity for large parties.

Crust

3   egg whites
½   cup sugar
½   teaspoon vanilla
21   Ritz crackers, crushed
⅔   cup chopped pecans

Filling

8   ounces cream cheese, softened
½   cup powdered sugar
     heavy cream, as needed

Topping

½   cup heavy cream, whipped
1   10-ounce can crushed pineapple, well drained
½   cup chopped pecans

Beat the egg whites until stiff and add sugar and vanilla. Fold crackers and pecans into egg white mixture. Press into greased 10″ pie pan. Bake at 350° for 30 minutes.

While crust is baking, prepare filling and topping. Mix cream cheese with powdered sugar (if mixture is too dry, add heavy cream as needed). Spread on cooled crust.

Top with whipped cream, sprinkle crushed pineapple over cream, and top it off with pecans. Chill until ready to serve. (This crust is delicious with other fillings, as well!)

Coronation Chicken

Serves: 8
Prepare: 10 minutes
Cook: 20 minutes

This recipe is a modified version of one served to guests at the coronation of Queen Elizabeth II.

1	onion, finely chopped
1	tablespoon oil
1	tablespoon curry powder
1	generous teaspoon tomato paste
½	cup red wine
½	cup water
1	bay leaf
1	teaspoon sugar
	salt and freshly ground pepper to taste
1-2	slices lemon
	lemon juice to taste
2	tablespoons apricot preserves
2	cups mayonnaise
3	tablespoons lightly whipped cream
2	pounds chicken, cooked and diced

In a skillet, soften onion in heated oil for 3-4 minutes. Add the curry powder and cook gently 1-2 minutes longer. Add tomato paste, wine, water, and bay leaf. Bring to boil and add sugar, salt, pepper, lemon slices, and lemon juice. Simmer uncovered for 5-10 minutes. Strain and cool.

Combine mayonnaise and preserves and slowly blend with tomato/onion mixture. Adjust seasoning, then fold in whipped cream. Toss diced chicken in curry sauce and refrigerate.

This dish can be prepared a day ahead.

Chocolate Truffle Cake

Serves: 8-12
Prepare: 30 minutes
Bake: 15 minutes

Oh, so rich ....

12	ounces semisweet chocolate chips
6	tablespoons butter
2	tablespoons sugar
2	teaspoons flour
1	teaspoon hot water
2	teaspoons vanilla
3	eggs, separated
	pinch salt
½	pint heavy cream
1	teaspoon vanilla
2	tablespoons granulated sugar

Melt chocolate and butter in double boiler over boiling water. Add sugar, flour, water, and vanilla. Remove from heat and whisk in egg yolks one at a time. Cool.

Beat egg whites with salt until stiff but not dry. Fold into chocolate mixture.

Spread into buttered 8″ springform pan. Bake at 425° for 15 minutes.

While cake is cooling, whip cream until fluffy, adding vanilla and sugar. Serve cake garnished with dollops of whipped cream.

William Clayton Collection

DINNER D'ELEGANCE

· ONE ·

Tortellini with Sun-dried Tomatoes
Hearts of Palm Salad
Lemon Sorbet
Venison in Phyllo
Carrot Pecan Pudding
Green Beans à la Nicoise
Cream Puff Ring
Hillsborough Cordials

· TWO ·

Foggy Nog
Wild Mushroom Soup
California Salad
Grapefruit Sorbet
Holiday Goose
Turnip Purée
Château Potatoes
Zucchini with Pesto
French Mint

· OPTIONS ·

Scallops of Salmon in Green Sauce
Wild Rice and Bacon Pilaf
Herbed Lamb Dijon
Carrot Soufflé
Shrimp and Mushroom Salad
White Chocolate Mousse

Tortellini with Sun-dried Tomatoes

Serves: 8
Prepare: 45 minutes
Marinate: 1 hour

Easy to make and everyone will love it!

½	pound sun-dried tomatoes, packed in oil (can be purchased in gourmet food shops)
⅓	cup olive oil
1	tablespoon lemon juice
2	garlic cloves, crushed
½	teaspoon salt
1	teaspoon freshly ground pepper
½	pound marinated artichoke hearts, drained and quartered
¼	pound whole blanched almonds
1	pound egg or spinach tortellini, cooked and cooled

Drain and chop tomatoes, reserving 1 tablespoon of oil. Combine reserved oil, olive oil, lemon juice, garlic, salt, and pepper in a bowl. Stir in tomatoes, artichokes, almonds, and cooked tortellini, and marinate at room temperature for 1 hour before serving.

Hearts of Palm Salad

Serves: 8
Prepare: 20 minutes

A year-round salad.

Salad

1	16-ounce can hearts of palm, sliced
1	12-ounce can artichoke hearts in water, drained and quartered
3	avocados, cut into chunks
2	ribs celery, sliced diagonally butter lettuce leaves

Dressing

¼	cup red wine vinegar
½	tablespoon minced parsley
1	teaspoon minced onion
1	small garlic clove, minced
1	small shallot, minced
¼	teaspoon Dijon mustard
¼	teaspoon crumbled tarragon
¾	cup plus 2 tablespoons olive oil
1	egg yolk

Blend all dressing ingredients, except olive oil, in food processor or blender. While still running, add oil and process for one minute.

Place prepared salad ingredients on lettuce leaves in salad bowl. Pour dressing over salad and serve at once.

Lemon Sorbet

Serves: 8
Prepare: 30 minutes
Freeze: 5½ hours

This is better if made a day ahead. It will hold in the freezer for several weeks.

2	teaspoons unflavored gelatin
1¾	cups water
1	cup sugar
	grated peel of ½ lemon
½	cup fresh lemon juice
2	egg whites

Soften gelatin in ½ cup water. In small saucepan, combine ½ cup sugar and remaining 1¼ cups water. Bring to a boil and cook for 2 minutes. Add gelatin mixture, stirring until dissolved. Add lemon peel and juice. Pour into 8" square pan and freeze until slushy (about 1½ hours), stirring occasionally.

Beat egg whites until fluffy and foamy. Gradually add remaining sugar, beating until soft peaks form. Fold egg whites into lemon mixture. Freeze until firm, about 4 hours.

This looks very pretty served in lemon shells, garnished with fresh mint.

Venison in Phyllo

Serves: 8
Prepare: 1½ hours
Bake: 20 minutes

This dish may also be made with ground lamb or sirloin if venison is not available. Once baked, rolls may be frozen and reheated at a later date.

Venison Rolls

8	ounces wild rice
1½	tablespoons instant chicken bouillon, dissolved in 4 cups water
1	onion, chopped
2	tablespoons butter
1	pound ground venison
2	teaspoons garlic powder
2	whole eggs, beaten
1	package frozen phyllo dough, thawed (follow package directions)
½	cup melted butter

Sauce

4	tablespoons butter
¼	pound mushrooms, thinly sliced
2	tablespoons flour
1½	cups light cream
2	teaspoons instant chicken bouillon
2	teaspoons finely chopped fresh parsley
¼	cup extra dry vermouth

Cook wild rice until fully open in bouillon mixture. Set aside to cool.

Sauté onion in 1 tablespoon butter until soft. Add venison and cook until crumbly. Season with garlic powder. Set aside to cool.

Combine rice and venison and mix well. When completely cooled, mix in eggs.

Place a large serving-spoon-size portion of venison mixture on a sheet of phyllo dough, about ¼ the distance from the top of the sheet. Fold top of sheet over mixture, fold both sides in towards center, and carefully roll towards bottom of sheet, eggroll style. Repeat procedure until venison mixture is completely used.

Place rolls in large buttered baking dish. Do not crowd together. When all rolls are in place, brush lightly with melted butter and bake at 375° for 20 minutes or until lightly browned.

Make sauce while rolls bake: melt butter in large frying pan. Sauté mushrooms and add flour to thicken. Slowly add cream, stirring until sauce is thick and smooth. Stir in chicken bouillon and parsley. Thin sauce with vermouth to taste. Add more cream if desired to bring sauce to correct consistency.

To serve, place rolls on serving platter, spoon small amount of sauce on top, and garnish with pinch of parsley. Serve remaining sauce in a small bowl.

Carrot Pecan Pudding

Serves: 8
Prepare: 15 minutes
Bake: 1 hour

May be served as a vegetable dish or an autumn dessert.

2	cups cooked, mashed carrots
1	teaspoon salt
½	cup sugar
4	tablespoons butter
1	cup milk
3	eggs, well beaten
2	heaping tablespoons flour
1	teaspoon baking powder
¼	teaspoon cinnamon
½	cup chopped pecans

Mix all ingredients together well. Bake in a greased casserole at 350° for 1 hour. If not nicely browned on top, place under broiler for a minute or two.

Green Beans à la Nicoise

Serves: 6　　　　*These complement almost any menu.*
Prepare: 15 minutes
Cook: 25 minutes

¼　cup olive oil
1　onion, thinly sliced
1　cup canned plum tomatoes
½　green pepper, chopped
½　cup chopped celery
¼　cup water
1　teaspoon salt
¼　teaspoon freshly ground pepper
1　bay leaf
6　sprigs parsley
1　pound green beans, cooked until tender
　　and drained

In a skillet, heat oil. Add onion and cook until golden brown. Add remaining ingredients except beans. Simmer, uncovered, about 25 minutes. Add beans and continue to simmer until heated through.

Cream Puff Ring

Serves: 8-10　　　*This dessert will impress your guests*
Prepare: 30 minutes　*and you will be pleased with its ease*
Bake: 1 hour　　　　*of preparation.*
Chill: 2-3 hours

Ring

1　cup water
6　tablespoons unsalted butter, cut in small
　　pieces
　　pinch of salt
1　cup all-purpose flour, sifted
1　teaspoon sugar
4　large eggs
　　egg wash: 1 egg mixed with 1 teaspoon
　　water

Filling

2　cups heavy cream
½　cup powdered sugar
1　teaspoon vanilla
1　pint fresh strawberries or raspberries
6　ounces chocolate chips

Over moderate heat bring water, butter, and salt to a boil in a 1½ quart heavy saucepan. Simmer until butter is melted, then immediately remove from heat and stir in flour and sugar all at once. Beat vigorously until mixture leaves sides of pan. Return to moderate heat and stir 1-2 minutes until mixture holds together and begins to film the bottom of the pan.

Remove from heat and make a well in the center of flour mixture. Break 1 egg into center of well. Beat until egg is absorbed. Repeat with remaining eggs, until each is well absorbed (the 3rd and 4th eggs will be absorbed more slowly). The finished dough will be smooth and shiny. If you prefer, eggs may be combined, one at a time, with flour mixture in a food processor, using metal blade.

Trace a 9″ circle on a greased, floured baking sheet (or mark with pencil on a sheet of baker's parchment). Put dough in a pastry bag and, using the ¾″ tip, pipe dough in a circle. Pipe a second circle outside the first, making sure they touch all the way around. Pipe a third circle on top of the other two. (Or you may drop 3″ mounds of dough in a circle, but make sure they touch.) Brush ring lightly with egg wash.

Bake in upper third of 425° oven for 20 minutes. Reduce heat to 375° and bake 10-15 minutes longer or until the ring is golden brown.

Turn off oven, remove ring, cut slits in sides to let steam escape, and return to hot, *turned off* oven for 10 minutes, leaving door ajar.

Remove ring from oven and cut in half horizontally. Place top half on another sheet of parchment, cut side up. Scoop out any uncooked dough from insides.

Whip cream with sugar and vanilla until it forms stiff peaks. Reserve ¾ cup cream to decorate the top. Fill the cooled ring with remaining whipped cream. Save 12 nice berries for the top of the ring, slice remaining berries, and sprinkle them over cream filling. Place top of ring on bottom, being careful to match the halves.

Melt chocolate chips in double boiler and drizzle over top of ring. Chill until well set, 2-3 hours.

When cool, dollop whipped cream on top of the ring as numbers on a clock. Place one whole berry on top of each dollop. Refrigerate until ready to serve.

Cream filling variation: add ⅓ cup unsweetened cocoa powder and substitute 2 tablespoons Kahlua or crème de cacao for vanilla. Omit the berries.

For romantic occasions, pastry can be made in the shape of a heart, and whipped cream dollops can be garnished with strawberries sliced in half lengthwise so they resemble hearts.

Hillsborough Cordials

Serves: 8-10   *Nice for after-dinner sipping!*
Prepare: 15 minutes

3	eggs
1	tablespoon instant coffee granules
1	tablespoon vanilla
2	tablespoons chocolate syrup
½	cup Irish whiskey

Mix all ingredients in blender for 30 seconds, then add:

1	14-ounce can sweetened condensed milk
1	pint heavy cream
¾	cup Irish whiskey
½	cup Amaretto liqueur

Blend 2 minutes longer and serve in small mugs.

Foggy Nog

Yield: 50 4-ounce servings
Prepare: 20 minutes

A rich but wonderful treat with quite a punch.

24   eggs, separated
1½   cups sugar
3   quarts milk
1   quart cream
1   quart rum
1   quart brandy
     nutmeg

Beat egg yolks well with sugar. Whisk in milk, cream, rum, and brandy. Whip egg whites until they form soft peaks, then carefully fold into nog. Top each serving with a dash of nutmeg.

Wild Mushroom Soup

Serves: 6-8
Prepare: 15 minutes
Cook: 1¼ hours

Fanciful and rich, so keep servings small.

8   tablespoons sweet butter
2   cups finely chopped onions
2½   pounds mushrooms, thinly sliced
¾   cup Madeira wine
     salt and freshly ground pepper to taste
3   ounces fresh chanterelles or morels, thinly sliced
4   cups chicken stock
     small amount of heavy cream

Melt butter in a large pot. Add onions and cook, covered, until tender. Add mushrooms to onions and cook over low heat for 20 minutes, stirring often. Add wine and season with salt and pepper. Add chicken stock, bring to a boil, and simmer, covered, for 45 minutes over low heat.

Strain the soup, and put the solids in a blender. Add a small amount of liquid and purée until smooth. Return purée to soup pot with remaining liquid and reheat, stirring to blend well. If the soup is too thick, add cream to thin. Serve immediately.

California Salad

Serves: 8   *Light and different.*
Prepare: 15 minutes

Salad

1   head butter lettuce, torn into bite-size
     pieces
1   avocado, sliced
1   can sliced water chestnuts
1   4-ounce package slivered almonds

Dressing

1   onion, grated
1   teaspoon salt
1   tablespoon mustard
1   teaspoon celery seed
⅔   cup sugar
⅓   cup vinegar
1   cup salad oil

Assemble salad ingredients.

Combine dressing ingredients in food processor or blender and process until well blended.

Pour dressing over salad and toss.

Grapefruit Sorbet

Serves: 8-10   *A refreshing respite or a simple*
Prepare: 35 minutes   *dessert.*
Freeze: 24 hours

2   large pink grapefruits, peeled and
     sectioned
⅔   cup sugar
4   tablespoons crème de menthe
¼   cup water
     mint sprigs

Combine sugar, grapefruit, crème de menthe, and water in food processor. Transfer to an 8″ square pan and let stand for 30 minutes, then freeze for 4-24 hours. After frozen, process again until smooth. Refreeze 1½ hours longer.

Remove from freezer 10 minutes before serving. Serve in champagne glasses, garnished with sprigs of mint.

Holiday Goose

Serves: 6-8   *An elegant variation on the*
Prepare: 10 minutes   *traditional turkey.*
Roast: 3½ hours

1   9-pound goose (available frozen during the
     holidays)
3-4   tart green apples, cored and diced
1   pound large pitted prunes

Stuff goose with apples and prunes and roast about 3½ hours at 325°. Drain off fat with turkey baster every 20-30 minutes and prick skin all over with fork. During last hour, baste goose with some of the fat to crisp skin. *Save the fat* (goose fat is a high-quality fat that freezes well).

Present goose on a platter surrounded by apples and prunes.

Turnip Purée

Serves: 8
Prepare: 30 minutes
Bake: 30 minutes

An excellent accompaniment to grilled or roasted fowl.

2 pounds carrots, peeled and sliced
1 pound turnips, peeled and diced
4 tablespoons butter, cut into pieces
  salt and freshly ground pepper to taste
  nutmeg, finely grated

Cook carrots and turnips separately in boiling, salted water until tender; about 10 minutes. Drain thoroughly. Add cooked vegetables in small batches to food processor and process until smooth, scraping sides of bowl frequently. Gradually add butter to purée. Add salt, pepper, and nutmeg to taste.

Place in 1-quart buttered casserole. Cover top with buttered waxed paper. Set in pan of hot water and bake at 350° for 30 minutes.

Château Potatoes

Serves: 8
Prepare: 10 minutes
Bake: 1 hour

Simply different.

8 baking potatoes, peeled
3 tablespoons butter, melted
  salt to taste
  freshly grated Parmesan cheese to taste

Thinly slice potatoes crosswise, leaving the bottom ⅓ intact. This will give a fan-like appearance when baked.

Place potatoes in well-greased baking dish and brush with butter. Bake at 400° for 1 hour. Brush potatoes with melted butter every 20 minutes. On last brushing, sprinkle potatoes with salt and Parmesan cheese. When done, potatoes should be tender and golden brown.

To be earthy (and for nutrition's sake), you may leave potatoes unpeeled.

Zucchini with Pesto

Serves: 8
Prepare: 45 minutes
Cook: 10 minutes

You may use frozen pesto for this, but fresh is best.

Pesto

3   bunches fresh basil
4   large garlic cloves, minced
¼   cup pine nuts
½   cup olive oil
½   teaspoon salt
¼   cup freshly grated Parmesan cheese

Zucchini

4   tablespoons unsalted butter
2   tablespoons olive oil
6-8   medium zucchini, grated
½   cup frozen or homemade pesto
    salt and freshly ground pepper to taste

To make pesto, process basil in a food processor or blender. Add garlic and pine nuts and process again. While processing, add olive oil in a slow steam, then add Parmesan cheese and salt.

Melt butter and oil in a skillet over medium heat. Add grated zucchini and sauté for 3-4 minutes or until just tender.

Add the pesto, increase heat and sauté for 1-2 minutes more. Add salt and pepper to taste and serve.

French Mint

Serves: 10-12
Prepare: 30 minutes
Freeze: 3-4 hours

This is wonderfully rich, so slice it thin!

1   pound butter, softened
4   cups powdered sugar
8   ounces unsweetened chocolate squares, melted
8   eggs
1½   teaspoons peppermint extract
2   cups chopped pecans

Beat butter and sugar together for 15 minutes. Add cooled, melted chocolate and beat 5 minutes more. Add eggs one at a time. Fold in peppermint extract. Sprinkle pecans on bottom of springform pan and pour mixture over nuts. Freeze for 3-4 hours or longer.

Remove from freezer 15 minutes before serving. Unmold and slice, inverting so pecans are on top.

Scallops of Salmon in Green Sauce

Serves: 6
Prepare: 20 minutes
Cook: 1 minute

An easy and elegant way to serve this beautiful fish.

Green Sauce

4 large leaves romaine lettuce
2 cloves garlic
1 tablespoon capers
¼ cup cilantro
3 tomatillos
2 serrano chilies

Salmon

1 3-pound fillet of salmon, skinned and boned
1-2 tablespoons oil
fresh cilantro

Purée all sauce ingredients in food processor until smooth, then season with salt and pepper.

Slice salmon into ½" thick slices. Heat oil over medium-high heat in nonstick skillet and sauté salmon, in 2 batches, 30 seconds on one side, 20 seconds on the other.

Spoon sauce over salmon and serve garnished with fresh cilantro.

Wild Rice and Bacon Pilaf

Serves: 4
Prepare: 20 minutes
Cook: 50 minutes

A savory pilaf with an elegant twist.

8 ounces wild rice
3 shallots, chopped
3 tablespoons butter
3 slices of bacon, cooked crisp and crumbled
freshly ground pepper to taste
2½ ounces chicken broth
1 bay leaf

Rinse rice thoroughly. Sauté shallots in butter. Add bacon and pepper. Stir in rice.

Put in ovenproof casserole and add chicken broth. Top with bay leaf. Bake, uncovered, at 450° for 50 minutes.

Herbed Lamb Dijon

Serves: 8
Prepare: 10 minutes
Roast: 30 minutes
per pound

A tantalizing aroma and hearty gravy make this a great leg of lamb.

½ cup Dijon mustard
3 tablespoons butter, melted
4 cloves of garlic, crushed
½ teaspoon thyme
½ teaspoon rosemary
1 large leg of lamb
2 tablespoons cornstarch
½ cup cold water
1 14½-ounce can beef broth

Combine mustard, melted butter, garlic, thyme, and rosemary. Coat lamb with mixture.

Roast lamb at 350° until meat thermometer registers 160° (for medium), or 170° (well done). Remove lamb to warm platter and cover. Degrease pan juices, reserving 1 tablespoon of fat.

Mix cornstarch with water. Add to lamb juices, beef broth, and reserved fat. Simmer until mixture thickens, stirring constantly.

Carrot Soufflé

Serves: 12
Prepare: 30 minutes
Bake: 45 minutes

Adds great color and taste to special menus.

3 cups carrots, cut into 2″ pieces
⅓ cup butter
3 eggs, lightly beaten
½ cup sugar
⅔ cup flour
2 teaspoons baking powder
¼ teaspoon salt
¼ cup orange juice

Cook carrots, covered, in boiling, salted water until tender (about 10-15 minutes). Drain, then mash or purée in food processor.

Add butter, eggs, and sugar; then flour, baking powder, salt, and orange juice, blending well. Pour into greased square pan or casserole. Bake at 375° for 45 minutes or more, until golden and puffy.

Shrimp and Mushroom Salad

Serves: 8 *Crispy, crunchy, fresh …*
Prepare: 20 minutes

Salad

20	shrimp, cleaned and deveined
¼	cup white wine
16	snow peas
10	mushrooms, thinly sliced
½	cup chopped macadamia nuts
3	tablespoons minced red onion
8	leaves bibb or butter lettuce

Dressing

2	tablespoons Dijon mustard
¼	cup fresh lime juice
2	tablespoons fresh dill (or 2 teaspoons dry)
1	cup good quality olive oil
	salt and freshly ground pepper to taste

Poach shrimp in white wine for about 3 minutes. Drain and ice to cool. Slice 8 shrimp lengthwise to the tail and reserve for garnish. Chop remaining shrimp and set aside. Blanch snow peas 2-3 minutes, drain, and ice to cool.

Combine shrimp pieces, snow peas, mushrooms, nuts, and onions in a bowl. Combine all ingredients for the dressing and shake well. Pour desired amount of dressing over shrimp mixture and toss well.

Place lettuce on individual salad plates and top with salad mixture. Garnish with extra shrimp.

White Chocolate Mousse

Serves: 10-12 *As lovely as it sounds.*
Prepare: 45 minutes
Chill: 3 hours

8	ounces white chocolate, broken into small pieces
½	cup unsalted butter
6	eggs, separated, at room temperature
1	cup powdered sugar, sifted
½	cup Frangelico liqueur
2	cups heavy cream
	grated dark chocolate for garnish

Melt white chocolate with butter in a saucepan, stirring constantly. Set aside.

Beat egg yolks, sugar, and liqueur until mixture is thick and creamy. Pour mixture into the top of a double boiler and cook over simmering water, whisking constantly, until very thick, about 3 minutes.

Remove to a large mixing bowl. Whisk in white chocolate mixture and stir until smooth and cool.

Beat cream until peaks are stiff. In a separate bowl, using clean beaters, beat the egg whites until stiff but not dry. Gently fold egg whites into the chocolate mixture; then fold in whipped cream. Refrigerate, covered, until set, about 3 hours.

Spoon the chilled mousse into individual sherbet glasses or goblets. Sprinkle with grated chocolate.

Cole Car Company

COUNTRY CLUB COCKTAILS

·ONE·

Cheese Boxes
Baked Bacon
Smoked Salmon Rolls
Barbecued Chicken Wings
Kipper Pâté
Grapes with Roquefort
Sherried Lobster Canapés
Crab Mousse
Josephinas
Shrimp Mousse

·TWO·

Shrimp Dip
Pesto Cheesecake
Hot Crab Dip
Brandied Brie
Caviar Pie
Grab Bag Hors d'Oeuvres
Salmon and Caviar Checkerboard
Chicken Liver Pâté
Tyroppitas

Cheese Boxes

Yield: 40 squares
Prepare: 1 hour
Bake: 15 minutes

A marvelous make-ahead hors d'oeuvre.

1 cup butter, softened
½ pound New York sharp cheddar cheese, grated
½ teaspoon salt
¼ teaspoon Tabasco
1 egg white
2 loaves French or sourdough bread

Beat butter, cheese, salt, and Tabasco together, then add egg white and mix well. Trim the crust off 2 loaves of French bread and cut into 1½" cubes.

Ice all sides of the bread cubes with cheese mixture except for the bottom. Bake at 375° for 15 minutes.

To freeze, place unbaked, iced bread cubes on a cookie sheet lined with waxed paper. Freeze solid, then remove to plastic bags, seal, and refreeze. For spur-of-the-moment hors d'oeuvres, they may be popped into the oven while still frozen. Bake at 375° for 15-20 minutes or until cheese is bubbly.

Baked Bacon

Serves: 20
Prepare: 20 minutes
Bake: 20 minutes

This dish can be frozen ahead of time and then baked.

2 eggs, beaten
1 teaspoon dry mustard
½ teaspoon cayenne pepper
2 teaspoons vinegar
10 thick bacon slices, quartered
2-3 cups finely crushed soda cracker crumbs

Combine eggs, mustard, pepper, and vinegar. Dip bacon slices first into egg mixture and then into crumbs. Arrange in single layer on rack in rimmed cookie sheet. Bake at 400° for 15-20 minutes until crisp. Serve hot from the oven.

Smoked Salmon Rolls

Serves: 20
Prepare: 15 minutes

A simple and delicious appetizer.

14 dill pickle spears
8 ounces cream cheese, softened
½ pound smoked salmon slices

Cut pickle spears into thirds lengthwise. Cut smoked salmon slices in half, spread each slice with cream cheese, and wrap around pickle spear. Anchor with toothpicks, and arrange on a platter, garnished with parsley.

Barbecued Chicken Wings

Serves: 8
Prepare: 30 minutes
Cook: 1 hour

Easy to eat and everyone will enjoy.

3	pounds chicken wings
	salt and freshly ground pepper to taste
¼	cup oil
1	cup honey
½	cup soy sauce
½	clove garlic
2	tablespoons tomato catsup

Remove wing tips and discard. Cut each wing into two parts.

Sprinkle with salt, pepper, and oil and set aside.

Combine remaining ingredients and pour over chicken. Place chicken in a greased shallow baking dish in a single layer.

Bake at 325° for 1 hour or until chicken is thoroughly cooked and sauce is caramelized.

Kipper Pâté

Serves: 8
Prepare: 20 minutes

This may be prepared in advance; it keeps well in the refrigerator.

8	ounces kipper fillets (canned kippers may be used but fresh kippers give a much better flavor)
6	ounces cream cheese, softened
4	tablespoons butter, melted
5	ounces heavy cream
	freshly ground pepper to taste

Blend all ingredients well and chill. The pâté can be served with crackers or on small pieces of celery.

Grapes with Roquefort

Serves: 10　　*Great with cocktails.*
Prepare: 30 minutes
Bake: 5 minutes
Chill: overnight

1	10-ounce package walnuts, finely chopped
1	8-ounce package cream cheese, softened
2	ounces Roquefort cheese
2	tablespoons heavy cream
1	pound seedless green grapes

Toast nuts in 275° oven until light brown, chop, and spread on a platter.

Combine cheeses and cream and mix until smooth.

Stir grapes into cheese mixture, then roll, one at a time, in toasted walnuts. Chill until ready to serve.

Sherried Lobster Canapés

Serves: 8-12　　*Wonderful and tasty!*
Prepare: 15 minutes

1	pound cooked lobster meat
¾	cup each: mayonnaise and sour cream, or to taste
1	tablespoon sherry
1	tablespoon lemon juice
	salt and freshly ground pepper to taste
1	tablespoon chopped parsley
	onion powder to taste
1	sourdough baguette
	sliced olives or pimento strips (optional)

Break lobster meat up with a fork until it is finely shredded. Add enough mayonnaise and sour cream to attain a good spreading consistency. Add sherry, lemon juice, salt and pepper, and chopped parsley. Mix thoroughly and season with onion powder to taste.

Slice the baguette into ½″ thick slices. Spread each slice with lobster mixture. Garnish with sliced olives or pimentos.

Crab Mousse

Yield: 4 cups　　*Very pretty served in a fish mold.*
Prepare: 20 minutes
Chill: overnight

1	envelope unflavored gelatin
3	tablespoons water
1	10-ounce can cream of mushroom soup
12	ounces cream cheese, softened
½	pound fresh crab meat
½	cup chopped celery
1	green onion, chopped

Soften gelatin in water. Heat soup and add gelatin mixture. Let cool, then add cream cheese, crab, celery, and green onion, and mix well.

Pack into well-greased, 4-cup mold and chill overnight.

When ready to serve, unmold and serve with melba rounds.

Josephinas

Serves: 20
(50 rounds)
Prepare:
30-40 minutes
Broil: 5 minutes

You'll never serve enough!

5	French rolls
½	pound butter, softened
1	cup canned green chilies, chopped
1	clove garlic, crushed
1¼	cups mayonnaise
¾	pound Monterey jack cheese, grated

Cut French rolls into ¼″ slices. Toast in oven on one side only. Mix butter, chilies, and garlic and spread on untoasted side of bread. Mix mayonnaise and cheese and spread on each round, being sure to entirely cover bread.

Broil until brown and fluffy; about 5 minutes. Serve immediately.

Shrimp Mousse

Serves: 15-20
Prepare: 30 minutes
Chill: 4 hours

This mousse is also good as a small luncheon salad.

1	10-ounce can condensed tomato soup
8	ounces cream cheese, sliced
2	envelopes unflavored gelatin
½	cup cold water
¾	pound bay shrimp, minced
¼	cup grated onion
¾	cup chopped celery
1	cup mayonnaise
1	tablespoon lemon juice
¼	teaspoon salt
½	teaspoon freshly ground pepper
	parsley sprigs, watercress, lemon slices
	assorted crackers

Heat soup and cream cheese in a double boiler over gently boiling water. Stir the mixture to blend thoroughly. Dissolve gelatin in cold water, add to hot soup mixture, and blend well.

Cool to room temperature. When completely cool, add shrimp, onion, celery, mayonnaise, lemon juice, salt, and pepper. Blend thoroughly and pour into a 5-cup decorative mold. Chill in the refrigerator for 4 hours (can be chilled overnight).

When ready to serve, unmold on chilled serving plate and garnish with parsley, watercress, and lemon slices. Serve with a basket of assorted crackers.

Shrimp Dip

Serves: 10
Prepare: 20 minutes

An ideal recipe for unexpected guests ... so always keep a can of shrimp in your larder!

1 cup mayonnaise
½ teaspoon Beau Monde seasoning
1 teaspoon Tabasco sauce
1 4-ounce can shrimp, minced
3 ribs celery, minced
½ onion, minced
4 green onions, minced

Combine ingredients and serve with chips or crackers.

Pesto Cheesecake

Serves: 12
Prepare: 45 minutes
Bake: 1¼ hours

A refreshing change from the usual pesto-pasta dish.

¼ cup fine bread crumbs, lightly toasted
¼ cup freshly grated Parmesan cheese
2½ cups fresh basil leaves
½ cup parsley sprigs, stemmed
¼ cup olive oil
½ teaspoon salt
1 garlic clove, halved
1 pound ricotta cheese, at room temperature
1 pound cream cheese, at room temperature
½ pound Parmesan cheese, freshly grated
4 eggs
⅓ cup pine nuts, lightly toasted
 whole basil leaves for garnish

Mix bread crumbs and ¼ cup Parmesan cheese. Sprinkle mixture into buttered 9″ springform pan, shaking to coat completely. Refrigerate.

Process basil leaves, parsley, oil, salt, and garlic in food processor until smooth paste forms, about 1 minute. Transfer to large bowl.

Blend ricotta, cream cheese, and ½ pound Parmesan cheese in food processor until smooth. Mix eggs, cheese mixture, and basil mixture until well blended. Pour into pan and sprinkle with pine nuts.

Set pan on baking sheet and bake at 325° for 1¼ hours. Turn oven off and cool cheesecake about 1 hour with door ajar. Transfer to rack and remove springform. Serve at room temperature, garnished with basil leaves. Serve with fresh, crusty French bread or crispy crackers.

Hot Crab Dip

Yield: 3 pints
Prepare:
20-30 minutes

A tasty hors d'oeuvre which can be made ahead and frozen until needed.

3   8-ounce packages cream cheese, softened
½   cup mayonnaise
2   teaspoons mustard
½   cup sauterne wine
½   teaspoon powdered sugar
1   teaspoon lemon juice
1   dash seasoning salt
3   cups crab meat

Combine all ingredients except crab, blending thoroughly, then fold in crab. Heat in a double boiler. Serve hot in a chafing dish with crisp crackers on the side.

Brandied Brie

Serves: 8-10
Prepare:
5-10 minutes
Broil: 3 minutes

Simply irresistible.

2   tablespoons butter
¼   cup sliced toasted almonds
1   tablespoon brandy
1   12-ounce round of Brie

Melt butter and combine with brandy and almonds. Keep mixture hot while preparing cheese.

Place the Brie in a shallow round casserole, or on a piece of foil with its edges pleated to form a shallow pan. Broil cheese for 3 minutes or until bubbly.

Pour brandy/butter mixture over hot cheese and serve immediately with water crackers.

Caviar Pie

Serves: 10-12
Prepare: 20 minutes
Chill: 2-3 hours

An elegant yet easy appetizer.

8   ounces cream cheese, softened
2-3   tablespoons finely chopped onion
1   tablespoon fresh lemon juice
4   tablespoons butter, melted
2   hard-boiled eggs, finely chopped
      finely chopped green onion to taste
1   2-ounce jar caviar

Line a pie plate or mold with plastic wrap. In a food processor, thoroughly blend cream cheese, onion, lemon juice, and butter. Pour into the mold and refrigerate until firm.

Unmold onto serving plate and layer top with chopped egg, onion, and caviar. Serve with crackers.

Grab Bag Hors d'Oeuvres

Serves: 12   *A tangy, crunchy treat.*
Prepare: 15 minutes
Chill: overnight

Dip

2	cups mayonnaise
½	cup sour cream
2	tablespoons horseradish
½	teaspoon Accent
2	teaspoons dry mustard
½	teaspoon salt
1	tablespoon lemon juice

Vegetables

1	cup cherry tomatoes
1	cucumber, cut into 1″ cubes
1	cup marinated artichokes hearts, drained
1	green pepper, cut into 1″ pieces
1	cup water chestnuts
1	avocado, cut into 1″ pieces
1	cup whole fresh mushrooms
1	cup shrimp or cooked chicken livers (optional)

Mix dip ingredients together well and chill overnight. Arrange vegetables on large platter and serve with tooth picks.

Salmon and Caviar Checkerboard

Serves: 20   *Easy to make ... pretty to serve.*
Prepare: 20 minutes

10	slices wholewheat bread
10	slices white bread
1	3-ounce package cream cheese, softened
2-3	tablespoons heavy cream
	freshly ground black pepper to taste
½	pound smoked salmon, thinly sliced
¼	cup butter, softened
4	ounces caviar
	juice of 1 lemon
	parsley sprigs for garnish

Trim crusts from bread so slices are uniformly square. Beat cream cheese with enough cream to make a soft mixture and spread on wholewheat bread. Sprinkle with pepper and top each slice with salmon.

Spread white bread slices with creamed butter, then with caviar, and sprinkle with lemon juice.

Cut each slice of bread into quarters and arrange salmon and caviar squares alternately in a checkerboard pattern on a large platter. Surround with parsley sprigs.

Chicken Liver Pâté

Yield: 3 cups   *Incredibly simple for such a*
Prepare: 30 minutes   *sophisticated dish!*
Chill: overnight

½   pound mushrooms
1   pound chicken livers
1   teaspoon garlic salt
1   teaspoon paprika
⅓   cup finely chopped green onions
¼   cup butter
⅓   cup dry white wine
    sprinkle of dill
3   drops Tabasco
½   cup butter, softened
    salt to taste

Gently sauté mushrooms, chicken livers, garlic salt, paprika, and green onions in ¼ cup butter for 5 minutes. Add wine, dill, and Tabasco. Cover and cook over low heat for 5-10 minutes more.

Cool and purée mixture until smooth in a blender or food processor. Blend in softened butter and salt to taste.

Chill overnight. Serve with small bread rounds or crackers.

Tyroppitas

Serves: 12   *Very popular cocktail treat.*
Prepare: 45 minutes
Bake: 15 minutes

8   ounces ricotta cheese
¼   pound feta cheese, grated
2   eggs
¼   teaspoon cayenne pepper
1   pound phyllo pastry, thawed (follow
    package directions)
½   pound butter, melted

Process cheeses, eggs, and cayenne pepper in food processor or blender until smooth.

Cut thawed phyllo into 2″ strips. Keeping unused portion covered, brush a strip with butter and place 1 teaspoon filling on bottom of strip. Roll up as you would a flag, forming a triangle. Place tyroppitas on a cookie sheet and brush with butter.

They may be frozen at this point or baked at 400° for 15 minutes, until brown. Serve hot.

Weatherford Collection

Sponsored by David, Judy, John and Derek Standridge

Family Affair

· ONE ·
Greek Spinach Pie
Apple Jelly-glazed Brisket
Carrot Salad
Chocolate Peanut Butter Pizza

· TWO ·
Creamed Vegetable Soup
California Brunswick Stew
Cucumber and Grape Salad
Chocolate Mint Pies

· OPTIONS ·
Tortilla Soup
Fried Shrimp with Walnuts
Marinated Spareribs
Seafood Lasagna
Bobby's Pasta Salad

Greek Spinach Pie

Serves: 12
Prepare:
30-45 minutes
Bake: 35 minutes

This may be partially baked, then frozen. Defrost and heat until cooked through—puffy and golden!

¼ cup finely chopped onion
¼ cup butter
3 10-ounce packages frozen chopped spinach, thawed and squeezed dry
3 eggs
½ pound feta cheese, crumbled
¼ cup chopped parsley
2 tablespoons chopped fresh dill or 1½ teaspoons dried dill
1 teaspoon salt
⅛ teaspoon white pepper
¾ cup butter, melted
½ 1-pound package phyllo dough, thawed according to package directions

Sauté onion in ¼ cup butter until golden; about 5 minutes. Combine spinach with onion and remove from heat. In a large bowl, beat eggs, then stir in cheese, parsley, dill, salt, pepper, and spinach-onion mixture. Mix well.

Brush a 9″ x 13″ baking dish lightly with some of the melted butter. Layer 8 phyllo sheets in bottom of dish, brushing each sheet with butter. (Keep unused sheets covered with a damp towel.) Spread the spinach mixture evenly over layered phyllo. Layer the remaining eight leaves, brushing each with melted butter. Drizzle remaining butter on top. Trim any uneven edges with scissors. Cut through top pastry layer to form 2″ x 3″ rectangles.

Bake at 350° for 30-35 minutes until top crust is puffy and golden. Serve warm. This may be used as a light main course or side dish.

Apple Jelly-glazed Brisket

Serves: 8
Prepare: 30 minutes
Chill: overnight
Bake: 3½, 1 hour

A great way to make an inexpensive cut of beef look and taste elegant.

Brisket

1 5-pound beef brisket
1 onion, quartered
3 tablespoons minced green onion
2 large garlic cloves, halved

Sauce

⅓ cup white wine
1 10-ounce jar apple jelly
3 tablespoons Dijon mustard
1 teaspoon salt
¾ teaspoon freshly ground pepper
¾ teaspoon curry powder

The day before serving, place brisket, onion, and garlic in a Dutch oven. Add ½″ water to pan. Cover and cook for approximately 3½ hours at 325°.

Drain liquid and discard onions and garlic. Scrape fat from top of brisket and discard.

To make the sauce, combine wine, jelly, mustard, curry, salt, and pepper in a saucepan. Stir over medium heat until jelly melts.

Slice brisket diagonally and cover with sauce. Let cool. Cover and refrigerate overnight.

Prior to serving, uncover and reheat brisket for 1 hour at 325°. Serve on a large warmed platter garnished with watercress bouquets.

Carrot Salad

Serves: 12   *A pretty salad the whole family will*
Prepare: 15 minutes   *enjoy.*
Marinate:
30 minutes

> 2   pounds carrots, peeled and grated
> ½   cup raisins
> ¼   cup raspberry vinegar
> ¾   cup olive oil
>   dash of cinnamon
>   salt and freshly ground pepper to taste
>   mint or parsley for garnish

Soak raisins in vinegar for 30 minutes, then combine with carrots.

Whisk vinegar with oil, then add cinnamon, salt, and pepper and toss with the carrots.

Serve garnished with mint or parsley to provide an appetizing color contrast.

Chocolate Peanut Butter Pizza

Serves: 20   *Everyone loves the shape—kids in*
Prepare: 20 minutes   *particular!*
Bake: 18 minutes

> ½   cup sugar
> ½   cup brown sugar, tightly packed
> ½   cup butter, softened
> ½   cup peanut butter
> ½   teaspoon vanilla
> 1   egg
> 1½   cups flour
> 2   cups miniature marshmallows
> 1   6-ounce package semisweet chocolate chips

Combine sugar, brown sugar, butter, peanut butter, vanilla, and egg in a large bowl and blend well. Stir in flour to form dough.

Press dough evenly into 12" x 14" pizza pan, forming a rim around the edge. Bake at 375° for 10 minutes.

Remove from oven and sprinkle with marshmallows and chocolate chips. Return to oven and continue baking 5-8 minutes more, or until marshmallows are puffy and lightly browned.

Cool and cut into wedges.

Creamed Vegetable Soup

Serves: 12
Prepare: 1 hour
Cook: 1 hour

This can also be made without cream. Either way, the children will love it.

¾ cup butter
¾ cup sliced onion
¾ cup peeled and chopped tomatoes
¾ cup sliced carrots
¾ cup sliced leek
¾ cup sliced green beans
¾ cup sliced zucchini
1½ cups diced potatoes
2 cloves garlic, minced
1½ teaspoons sugar
1½ quarts chicken stock
½ cup heavy cream
  salt and freshly ground pepper to taste
  chopped fresh parsley

Melt butter in large stock pot over medium-high heat. Add onion and sauté 1-2 minutes. Reduce heat to low, add remaining vegetables and sugar, and cook until vegetables are soft but not brown; about 30 minutes. Add stock and bring to boil over medium-high heat. Reduce heat and simmer about 10 minutes. Let cool slightly.

Transfer to blender or food processor in batches and purée until smooth. Taste and adjust seasoning. Return to stock pot, place over medium heat, and gradually stir in cream. Heat through but do not boil. Garnish each serving with chopped fresh parsley.

If preparing ahead, soup may be chilled or frozen before cream is added. Be sure soup is warm before combining with cream.

California Brunswick Stew

Serves: 8
Prepare:
25-30 minutes
Cook: 4 hours

A hearty meal in itself; in smaller portions it becomes an excellent side-dish!

1 pound ground beef
1 pound ground pork
1 16-ounce can tomatoes
1 16-ounce can corn
2 large bell peppers, finely chopped
2 large onions, finely chopped
1 cup catsup
1 6-ounce can tomato paste
2 tablespoons Worcestershire sauce
½ cup barbecue sauce
1 clove garlic
½ cup butter
  salt and freshly ground pepper to taste

Brown beef and pork, drain fat, then combine with remaining ingredients in a large pot. Cover and simmer over low heat for 4 hours, stirring often.

Cucumber and Grape Salad

Serves: 6
Prepare: 20 minutes
Marinate:
30 minutes or more
Chill: 3-4 hours

Very pretty ... refreshing appearance and taste.

Marinade

3   tablespoons olive oil
1   tablespoon wine vinegar
¼   teaspoon salt
¼   teaspoon freshly ground pepper
1   teaspoon prepared mustard

Salad

1   large English cucumber, peeled and thinly sliced
1   pound seedless green grapes, halved
1½   cups water
1   3-ounce package lemon jello
3   tablespoons orange juice
5   tablespoons lemon juice
1   tablespoon finely chopped onion
⅛   teaspoon cayenne pepper
½   teaspoon salt
¼   teaspoon freshly ground pepper
1   head iceberg lettuce, shredded

Place marinade ingredients in a bowl and beat well with a fork. Add grapes and cucumber slices and marinate at least 30 minutes or until ready to use.

Boil ¾ cup of the water, remove pan from heat, and add jello, stirring until completely dissolved. Stir in remaining water, juices, onion, cayenne, salt, and pepper. Cool until almost set.

Remove grapes and cucumbers from marinade with a slotted spoon, drain thoroughly, and add to jello, reserving some grapes and cucumbers, and the marinade, for garnish.

Pour jello into a 2-cup ring mold, cover with plastic wrap, and refrigerate until completely set.

Unmold and arrange lettuce around jello. Garnish with reserved grapes and cucumber, sprinkle with marinade, and serve immediately.

Chocolate Mint Pies

Serves: 20-25
Prepare: 40 minutes
Freeze: 5 hours

Easy and fun for the children to help put together.

Crust

2   cups vanilla wafer crumbs
¼   cup butter, melted

Filling

1   cup butter, softened
2   cups powdered sugar, sifted
4   squares unsweetened chocolate, melted
¾   teaspoon mint extract (or to taste)
2   teaspoons vanilla

For crust, mix wafer crumbs and melted butter. Press into bottom of foil muffin cups. Set aside.

Cream butter and sugar. Add melted chocolate and blend well. Mix in eggs, mint extract, and vanilla. Fill each cup and freeze until firm.

Remove from freezer 5 minutes before serving. Serve out of muffin cups, topped with a dollop of whipped cream.

These can be frozen for up to two months in a covered container. Fun for a pool party or barbecue!

Tortilla Soup

Serves: 20
Prepare: 20 minutes
Cook: 1¾ hours

Festive in color and flavor; this can spark that special occasion!

1   2-pound chicken plus 2 breasts
6-7   quarts water
1   rib celery
1   carrot
1   onion, halved
3   16-ounce cans tomatoes
1   16-ounce can corn, drained
1   green pepper, finely chopped
1   large onion, chopped
1   4-ounce can sliced black olives, drained
2   teaspoons powdered cumin
3   tablespoons chili powder
2   cloves garlic, minced
1   tablespoon salt
½   head red cabbage, shredded
       tortilla chips
       grated cheddar cheese

Simmer chicken with celery, carrot, and onion in 7 quarts of water in a 10-quart stock pot for 1 hour. Remove chicken, discard vegetables, and strain broth. Remove meat from chicken bones and set aside.

Add remaining ingredients, except cabbage, to broth and simmer for 30 minutes. Add shredded cabbage and chicken pieces and simmer another 15 minutes.

To serve, place a handful of tortilla chips in a shallow soup bowl, ladle hot soup over, and cover generously with grated cheese.

Fried Shrimp with Walnuts

Serves: 8
Prepare: 45 minutes
Marinate:
30 minutes
Cook: 10 minutes

A very zippy dish; a nice change.

10	ounces fresh shrimp, cleaned
1½	teaspoons salt
1	tablespoon Chinese wine or vinegar
¼	teaspoon sesame oil
¼	teaspoon cornstarch
¼	teaspoon monosodium glutamate (optional)
	freshly ground pepper to taste
8	ounces walnuts
2	ounces green peas
1	carrot, cut in 1″ pieces
6	1″ slices fresh ginger
3	green onions, cut in 1″ pieces
	water for boiling
	oil for deep frying

Sauce

1½	teaspoons cornstarch
¼	teaspoon salt
1	teaspoon monosodium glutamate (optional)
	a few drops sesame oil
4	teaspoons water

Rub shrimp with 1 teaspoon salt, rinse, and pat dry. Combine remaining salt, vinegar, oil, cornstarch, monosodium glutamate, and pepper. Add shrimp and marinate for at least 30 minutes.

Boil walnuts in water for 10 minutes, then add 1 cup cold water and bring to the boil again. Drain immediately. Boil prawns in water until just pink, about 3 minutes. Blanch green peas.

Deep fry walnuts for 4 minutes, then set aside. Deep fry shrimp for 1½ minutes and set aside. Drain excess oil and stir fry carrot, ginger, onions, and peas quickly, about 1 minute. Add the wine and shrimp.

Combine sauce ingredients, pour into wok, and stir-fry thoroughly. Add walnuts, stir again, and serve.

Marinated Spareribs

Serves: 4
Prepare: 50 minutes
Marinate: overnight
Grill: 15 minutes

A Korean delight ... flank steak is equally wonderful done this way. Score the steaks before marinating.

2   pounds spareribs (beef or pork)
1   tablespoon peanut oil

Marinade
4   tablespoons soy sauce
3   garlic cloves, crushed
2   tablespoons Sake or dry white wine
4   tablespoons water
2   teaspoons roasted sesame seeds, ground
2   tablespoons sugar
1   teaspoon freshly ground pepper
4   green onions, chopped
1   onion, chopped
1   large ripe pear, peeled, cored, and finely chopped

Using a sharp knife, cut ribs so they will lie flat, then criss-cross meat and bone with small, deep incisions, taking care not to cut through the meat entirely.

To make the marinade, combine all ingredients in a large, shallow dish. Add the ribs, turning once or twice to coat, cover, and set aside to marinate overnight at room temperature.

Brush ribs lightly with oil and grill over moderately high heat for 30 minutes, or until they are cooked through and golden brown.

Seafood Lasagna

Serves: 12
Prepare: 1 hour
Bake: 40 minutes

A light variation on this traditional favorite.

8   ounces lasagna noodles
1   pound ricotta cheese
¾   cup chopped parsley
     salt and freshly ground pepper to taste
     dash of Tabasco
     pinch of nutmeg
2   cloves garlic, minced
4   eggs
4   tablespoons flour
4   tablespoons butter
1   cup hot milk
2   cups light cream
⅓   cup freshly grated Parmesan cheese
¾   pound mozzarella cheese, grated
1   pound shrimp, peeled and chopped
10   ounces bay scallops
8   ounces crab meat

Cook lasagna according to package directions. Drain and place in ice water; set aside.

Mix ricotta cheese, parsley, salt, pepper, Tabasco, nutmeg, garlic, and eggs. Set aside.

Make a roux with flour and butter. Add hot milk and cream. Cook over low heat for 5 minutes, stirring constantly. Sauce will be the consistency of thick cream.

Cover bottom of a 9″ x 13″ casserole with lasagna noodles. Spread ⅓ of ricotta mixture onto noodles, then add ⅓ of cheeses. Sprinkle ⅓ of seafood over cheeses. Cover with ⅓ of sauce. Repeat process. Top with a layer of noodles, sauce, cheeses, then seafood. Cover with foil. Bake at 350° for 40 minutes. Serve bubbling hot.

Bobby's Pasta Salad

Serves: 6-8   *A pretty side dish.*
Prepare: 20 minutes
Cook: 10 minutes

Salad

12	ounces shell macaroni
1	bunch fresh broccoli, florets only
4	carrots, peeled and julienned
1	jar marinated artichokes, drained
1	tomato, sliced
½	cup each diced red and green peppers (optional)

Dressing

½	cup olive oil
3	tablespoons lemon juice
1	small clove garlic, minced and mashed into ½ teaspoon salt
¼	teaspoon oregano
¼	teaspoon paprika
	freshly ground pepper to taste

Cook macaroni according to package directions, rinse with cold water, and drain well. Blanch broccoli florets and carrots. Lightly toss macaroni with all vegetables, and sprinkle with dressing.

To make dressing, combine all ingredients and allow to stand for a few minutes before using.

Blackhawk Collection

Sponsored by Marcia C. Wadell D.D.S., Practice limited to periodontics

RESTAURANT AND CATERER FAVORITES

MacArthur Park Catering
MacArthur Park
Judy Benton's Catering
Ciao
La Locanda
Bella Vista

Danish-French Catering
Clown Alley
Prego
Borel's
Firehouse Bar-B-Que
As You Like It

Woodlake Joe's
La Pinata
The Keeping Room
Alpine Inn
Nathan's
Le Boulanger
Velvet Turtle

Grilled Duck Breast

6   duck breasts, boned, skins pricked all over with fork
12   slices bacon, cooked crisp

Marinade

juice and zest of 2 oranges
12   leaves fresh sage, chopped
6   tablespoons virgin olive oil
½   cup red wine vinegar
6   bay leaves
1   tablespoon cracked black pepper

Braised Red Cabbage

¼   cup chopped apple-cured bacon (or regular bacon, if unavailable)
2   tablespoons butter
1   small head red cabbage, cored and thinly sliced
juice of 1 lemon
5   tablespoons red wine vinegar
3   tablespoons beef stock
1   tablespoon sugar (or to taste)
salt and freshly ground pepper to taste

LIVE MAINE LOBSTER
HEADED NORTH
ON BAYSHORE FREEWAY.

Marinate breasts several hours or overnight. Slowly grill over charcoal until desired doneness is reached, basting occasionally with marinade. When done, slice diagonally and arrange on top of hot cabbage.

To make cabbage, sauté bacon in butter till transparent, add cabbage and cook lightly. Add remaining ingredients and cook slowly, until cabbage is slightly limp but still crisp; about 4-5 minutes.

Garnish with fresh sage leaves, orange zest, and 2 slices of bacon. Serves 6.

Grilled Escarole, Smoked Ham, and Goat Cheese Appetizer

12   slices boneless smoked ham, 1/16" thick x 5" square
24   leaves of escarole
¾   cup grated goat cheese

Dressing

3   tablespoons vinegar
3   tablespoons orange juice
2   teaspoons stone-ground mustard
¼   teaspoon salt
¼   teaspoon cracked black pepper
⅔   cup olive oil

Spread approximately 1 tablespoon of cheese onto center of each piece of ham, then lay 2 leaves of escarole over the cheese and dribble a little dressing over all.

Roll up jelly-roll fashion, with ham on the outside. Secure with a toothpick.

Dip ends of each ham roll in dressing and grill over a slow fire.

To serve, remove toothpicks and place 2 ham rolls per person on serving plate, spoon some of the remaining dressing over the top. Serves 6.

Killer Chicken

8	½-pound chicken breasts, cut in half
½	cup oil
	seasoned flour (see below)
4	cloves garlic, crushed
4	large shallots, finely chopped
1	cup white wine
1	14½-ounce can chicken broth
	salt and freshly ground pepper to taste
¼	cup chopped parsley

Seasoned Flour

1	cup flour
½	cup cornstarch
1	teaspoon rosemary
1	teaspoon marjoram
2	teaspoons basil
½	teaspoon sage
1	teaspoon oregano
2	teaspoons tarragon
½	teaspoon Accent
1	teaspoon garlic powder
1	teaspoon thyme
½	teaspoon poultry seasoning
1	teaspoon seasoned salt

Coat chicken breasts in seasoned flour. Heat oil in frying pan. Add chicken, and fry slowly until golden. Salt and pepper to taste.

Remove chicken from pan. Set aside. Add chopped garlic and shallots to pan. Sauté until transparent. Add white wine and chicken broth and cook for 5 minutes longer.

Pour over chicken and bake, covered, at 350° for ½ hour. Sprinkle with chopped parsley before serving. Serves 8.

Paglia e Fieno

½   pound butter
1   pound fresh green peas
1   pound pancetta (or prosciutto), julienned
2   cups heavy cream
½   pound Parmesan cheese, freshly grated
½   pound each: egg and spinach noodles

If using pancetta, sauté pancetta, then pour off the grease. Add butter and melt, then add peas and sauté lightly. (If using prosciutto, melt butter and add the prosciutto with the peas.) Add the cream and reduce slightly while cooking the pasta in salted, boiling water until *al dente.* Add the cooked, drained pasta to the cream mixture, sprinkle with Parmesan, and toss lightly. Serve immediately. Serves 4.

You talk. You laugh. You drink. You watch the pastaio invent your Fettucine al Pesto Genovese. (The couple next to you has the charcoaled quail.) You order an Italian ice, a cappucino. 11 AM to midnight. Whatever, practically whenever. Ristorante Ciao. Nothing this side of Milan comes close.

230 Jackson Street, San Francisco, California
(415) 982-9500

Pasta Carbonara

200	grams (½ pound) pasta
2	thick slices Italian prosciutto, cut in pieces
1	cup fresh cream
2	egg yolks
	salt and white pepper to taste
30	grams (2 tablespoons) butter
50	grams (¼ cup) freshly grated Parmesan cheese

Boil pasta till *al dente*, drain, and dry thoroughly. Combine prosciutto, cream, egg yolks, salt, and pepper and add to pasta. Add butter, mix well, and serve with Parmesan cheese. Serves 2.

LA LOCANDA

The finest meats, vegetables, fish and cheeses.
Pasta made fresh daily.

Lunch: Tuesday-Friday, 11:30-2 p.m.
Dinner: Tuesday-Saturday, 5-10 p.m.; Sunday, 5-9 p.m.
(Closed Monday.)
Extensive wine list. Banquet facilities.
Your Hosts: Guido and Renzo.

1136 Broadway, Burlingame, California
(415) 347-1053

Veal Moutarde

12	ounces veal scallops
1	tablespoon butter
	flour
8	mushrooms, sliced
1	tablespoon shallots, minced
2	tablespoons sherry
1	tablespoon Dijon mustard
1	cup heavy cream
½	cup brown (meat) stock or brown sauce
	dash Worcestershire
1	tablespoon butter

Flour and lightly sauté veal scallops in butter 1 minute on each side. Add mushrooms, shallots, sherry, and mustard and stir to coat. Pour the cream over, then the brown sauce, Worcestershire, and the butter. Cook until sauce is reduced slightly. Serves 4.

—Courtesy of Chef José Sandoval

Bella Vista
Continental Cuisine

Dine in the Redwoods with a panoramic view of the East Bay Hills and the Bay.

13451 Skyline Boulevard, Woodside, California
(415) 851-1229

Gravlax "Danish-French" Style

7-8   pounds Norwegian salmon, skinned and boned

Marinade

½   cup coarse salt
4   teaspoons sugar
1   cup chopped dill
1   teaspoon crushed white pepper
½   cup Aquavit
1   teaspoon tarragon, chopped

Mustard Sauce

2   cups mayonnaise
⅓   cup pickling spice
2   teaspoons dry mustard

Gravlax is a Scandinavian-style salmon. It is pickled with sugar, salt, and lots of dill. For our version of this dish, we add Aquavit and crushed white pepper.

Place fillets in stainless steel pan, rub with marinade mixture, and pour remaining liquid over fish. Cover with coarse pepper; place another stainless steel pan over fish to provide pressure. Refrigerate one day.

Turn fillets over and refrigerate one more day. On third day, place 4-5 pounds of weight on top pan to provide additional pressure and refrigerate one more day.

Drain and save juices. Wrap fish in foil and place in freezer for 2-3 hours to ease slicing. Slice thinly and at an angle. Combine sauce ingredients and serve on the side. (This dish must be kept well refrigerated at all times.)

Danish-French Catering

Clown Alley Chili

2   pounds small red beans
4   pounds ground round or chopped sirloin
2   small onions
1   cup chili powder
1   large can diced tomatoes
1   can consomme
2   red bell peppers, chopped
   salt and freshly ground pepper to taste

Soak beans overnight and cook until barely tender. Set aside. Combine meat, onions, and chili powder and cook until meat is browned and onions are tender.

Add remaining ingredients and simmer for 30 minutes. Add beans to chili sauce and allow to cook for another 15 minutes.

Add 1-2 cups of water from bean pot to thicken chili—the longer it cooks the thicker the chili will become. Serves 6-8.

Would you believe we serve the best Hamburgers in the "City" … 24 hours a day. Steak sandwiches, Hot Dogs, French Fries, Milk Shakes, and more, too … no clowning around. It's terrific!!! Drop on by anytime.

42 Columbus Avenue, San Francisco, California
(415) 421-2540

Focaccia al Formaggio

Pizza Dough

½	cup lukewarm water
½	package active dry yeast
1	pound flour
1	tablespoon olive oil
½	teaspoon salt

Topping

10	ounces Gorgonzola cheese
	fresh oregano
	fresh sweet basil
	fresh parsley, chopped
5	scallions, chopped

To make dough, dissolve yeast in water. Add remaining ingredients and knead until dough is elastic. Allow to rest a few minutes before rolling out. (No risings are required).

Roll dough as thin as possible and place on greased pizza pan. Crumble cheese on top, sprinkle with herbs, green onion and a little extra virgin olive oil. Bake at 500° for 5 minutes, or until the Gorgonzola is melted and bubbly, and the crust is golden brown. Cut in small pieces and serve as an appetizer. Serves 6.

Pesce.
Pizza.
Pollo.
Pasta.

Cooking at Prego from midday 'til midnight.

2000 Union Street, San Francisco, California
(415) 563-3305

Seafood Gumbo

Stock

8 cups water
3 cups shrimp shells
2 ribs celery, sliced in 2" slices
½ large onion, peeled and quartered

Gumbo

¼	pound butter	1	teaspoon oregano
2	cups diced onion	1	bay leaf
2	cups diced celery	½	tablespoon Tabasco
2	cups diced bell pepper	3	tablespoons gumbo filé
1	tablespoon minced garlic	1	cup tomato sauce
2	teaspoons cayenne	½	cup tomato paste
2	tablespoons paprika	½	pound crab meat
1	tablespoon salt	½	pound shrimp, peeled
1	teaspoon white pepper		and deveined (use
1	teaspoon black pepper		51-60s or 71-90s)
1	teaspoon thyme	1	cup oysters with juice,
			shucked

To make stock, combine water, shrimp shells, celery, and onion. Bring to a boil. Remove from heat and let stand 30 minutes to extract flavor, then strain and set aside.

Melt butter, add onion, celery, and bell pepper, and sauté until onions are just turning translucent.

Add garlic, cayenne, paprika, salt, white and black peppers, thyme, oregano, bay leaf, Tabasco, and gumbo filé. Turn up flame and cook for 6 minutes, stirring constantly.

Add tomato sauce and tomato paste. Reduce heat and simmer for 5 minutes, stirring constantly.

Add stock and bring to a boil, then reduce heat and simmer for an hour. Add seafood and continue to simmer for 5 minutes longer. Remove from heat and serve immediately. Serves 8.

BOREL'S.

San Mateo's showcase restaurant ... with a spectacular view overlooking San Mateo and the Bay. Fresh seafood, Prime rib, steaks, lamb, veal, and pasta specialties. Piano music in the dining room Tuesday through Saturday evenings. Banquet seating to 150. Champagne buffet brunch every Sunday, only $11.95. Happy Hour Monday through Friday, 5-7 p.m. with complimentary hors d'oeuvres. Lounge entertainment every Friday and Saturday evening. Plenty of free parking.

Lunch: Monday-Friday, 11:30 a.m.-2:30 p.m.
Dinner: Monday-Thursday, 6-10 p.m.; Friday, 5:30-11 p.m.; Saturday, 5-11 p.m.; Sunday, 5-9:30 p.m.
Brunch: Sunday, 10:30 a.m.-2 p.m.
All major credit cards accepted. Reservations suggested.

2951 Campus Drive, San Mateo, California
(415) 341-7464

Oven-barbecued Shrimp

1   cup Firehouse Bar-B-Que sauce
2   pounds medium-sized shrimp, shelled and
     deveined hot flavorings to taste: cayenne,
     black pepper, tabasco (optional)
3   cups cooked white rice
3   tablespoons chopped fresh parsley

Heat barbecue sauce until it boils. If desired, add hot flavorings to sauce. Spread shrimp in a shallow baking pan and cover with heated sauce. Cover and marinate for several hours in the refrigerator.

Bake shrimp at 300° for 30 minutes, stirring several times while baking.

Mound rice on a serving platter and arrange shrimp on top. Sprinkle with parsley. Serve additional sauce on the side if desired.

Avocado Delight

6½ tablespoons water
2 packages unflavored gelatin

Egg Layer
6 hardboiled eggs, chopped
½ cup mayonnaise
¼ cup minced parsley
1 large green onion, minced
¾ teaspoon salt
6 dashes Tabasco
freshly ground pepper to taste

Avocado Layer
2 medium avocados, diced
1 medium avocado, puréed
1 large green onion, minced
3 tablespoons fresh lemon juice
2 tablespoons mayonnaise
½ teaspoon salt
2 tablespoons canned diced jalapeno peppers
2 tablespoons minced cilantro

Sour Cream Layer
1½ cups sour cream
¼ cup minced onion

Sprinkle gelatin over cold water, let stand a few minutes, then heat until melted.

Assemble ingredients for egg layer, then add 2 tablespoons gelatin mixture. Pour into 8″ or 9″ springform pan. Refrigerate while assembling avocado layer.

Mix all ingredients for avocado layer, adding 2 more table-

As You Like It

Fine catering for all occasions: special events, Luaus, international menus. Specializing in seminars and business meetings in the Monterey, Tahoe, and Clear Lake areas.

764 Polhemus Road, San Mateo, California
(415) 341-9394

spoons gelatin mixture. Pour on top of egg layer. Return to refrigerator.

Mix sour cream, onion, and remaining gelatin. Pour carefully over avocado layer. Allow to set at least 2 hours (can be prepared one day ahead).

When ready to serve, run a knife around edge of mold and remove sides of pan. Place on tray and surround with rye bread triangles. Garnish with twisted lemon slice and parsley. Serves 6-8.

Fresh Artichoke Frittata

3   small fresh artichokes
3   large eggs
3   cloves garlic, chopped very fine
1   ounce olive oil
    salt and freshly ground pepper to taste
    freshly grated Parmigiana cheese

Peel and trim artichokes and chop into quarter-size pieces. Put olive oil in a small skillet and heat slowly. When oil is hot, add chopped garlic. Be very careful with the cooking of the garlic as it tends to burn easily and turn bitter. When the garlic is just turning a light brown, add artichokes and sauté slowly until tender. Whip eggs and slowly add to artichokes, then add salt and pepper to taste and let the frittata cook slowly.

When it has firmed up, place the skillet in the oven for about 5 minutes at 350°. This will puff the frittata. Take the frittata from the oven and place on a dish, sprinkle a large amount of grated cheese on top as you serve it. Serves 6.

This recipe makes a wonderful lunch or brunch treat. It has been handed down to me by my mother who brought it to this country from the province of Tuscany in Italy.

Please enjoy,

Leo Giorgetti

Fiesta Chicken

Chicken

4	whole chicken breasts, boned, split, and skinned
½	cup finely chopped cilantro
4	fresh jalapeno peppers, finely chopped
3	slices bacon, cooked crisp and crumbled
4	tablespoons butter, softened
½	cup fine bread crumbs
½	cup freshly grated Parmesan cheese
¼	teaspoon freshly ground pepper
4	ounces Monterey jack cheese, cut into 8 strips (each ½″ x 1½″)

Salsa Fresca

½	green onion, finely chopped
2	avocados, chopped
8	tomatoes, chopped
2	bunches cilantro, finely chopped
4-5	fresh serrano chilies, finely chopped
	juice of 1 lemon or lime
	salt and freshly ground pepper to taste

Mexican Restaurant

1205 Burlingame Avenue, Burlingame, California
(415) 375-1070

Lightly pound breast meat between sheets of wax paper; set aside. Mix cilantro, jalapenos, crumbled bacon, and softened butter; set aside. Combine bread crumbs, Parmesan cheese, and pepper; set aside.

Spread ½ tablespoon butter mixture across each breast about 1″ from lower edge. Lay a strip of cheese over butter mixture. Fold lower edge of breast over filling then fold in sides and roll up to enclose filling, tucking in loose ends.

Dip each rolled breast in the melted butter, drain briefly, then roll in bread crumb mixture until evenly coated. Place chicken breasts seam side down in baking dish. Do not crowd. Cover and refrigerate for at least 4 hours (or place in freezer for about 30 minutes).

Bake uncovered at 425° for approximately 20-25 minutes. Do not turn chicken. (Do not worry if some of the filling seeps out).

For topping, combine all ingredients and mix well. Pour over chicken before serving, and serve extra salsa on the side. Serves 8.

Helpful hint: jalapeno cheese may be substituted for the Monterey jack and fresh jalapeno peppers.

Pecan Pasta

½ pound toasted pecans, coarsely chopped
1 pound fresh fettucine
6 tablespoons sweet butter, cut into ½" cubes
½ cup coarsely chopped Italian parsley (grow your own from seed ... easy and important)
1 cup freshly grated Parmigiano-Reggiano cheese (don't substitute)
1 cup heavy cream, at room temperature
   kosher salt and freshly ground black pepper

To toast pecans, place on cookie sheet in 325° oven for 10-15 minutes.

Cook pasta in boiling, salted (1 tablespoon) water for 2-5 minutes or until perfect. Drain and place in *large* bowl, add remaining ingredients (saving ½ the pecans and ½ the parsley for garnish). Toss and *taste* for salt and pepper ... it will require more salt than you expect. Serve on heated plates, garnished with remaining pecans and parsley. Serves 4 as an entrée or 8 as a first course.

The Keeping Room was established in 1978 by Barbara Thoreson and Lori Rutter, mother and daughter, who shared a dream to produce food in a restaurant that matched the quality, care, and character of good home cooks everywhere. We had no formal training when we began, but we were enthusiastic and wished only to learn, explore, and never compromise quality.

In our pursuit we treasured the influence of many fine teachers ... Combe, Pepin, Medrich, Bugialli, Kamman, Marshall, Hazan, Poore, Field, Aidells, Pancaldi, Kuhn.

Changes came ... full-time catering eclipsed the restaurant operation; in 1984, Lori moved on to other interests; the original location was sold in 1985 ... but my enthusiasm remained.

The Keeping Room now lives in an all-new catering kitchen, at 520 Warren Road in San Mateo ... my home—where I can keep a close eye on the fresh herbs growing in the back yard and tend to the flowers I use to garnish and decorate the things I make.

Catering is my business, but food is my passion, so I don't buy stocks and sauces and dressings—I make them. I don't buy breads and pastries and pasta—I make them. I make ice cream and, properly inspired, vinegars and fresh cheese and sausages— and I love every minute of it! Food has taught me respect and given me joy. That's what I bring to you.

520 Warren Road, San Mateo, California
(415) 343-7766

Spaetzle

3½ cups flour
1   teaspoon salt
3   eggs, slightly beaten
1   cup water

Put flour in a bowl; make a well; place salt, eggs, and water in well; and mix thoroughly. Put small amount of dough on a cutting board and snip off pieces with knife into boiling, salted water.

As spaetzle rises to top, scoop out with slotted spoon and put under cold running water. Dry in a colander.

To serve, melt a generous piece of butter in a heavy frying pan, add spaetzle, keep turning until slightly browned. Great served with Sauerbraten!

Alpine Inn
European Cuisine

The warm cozy atmosphere of the Alpine Inn is reminiscent of European charm. Werner Bertram and his wife Hedy extend to their guests a truly gracious hospitality. Their European cuisine includes such splendid entrées as Veal Dijonnaise, Sauerbraten, Red Cabbage, Spaetzle, and Fresh Fillet of Sole Bourgogne. Be sure to save room for their luscious chocolate mousse and other desserts. For a delightful dining experience, the Alpine Inn is a must.

Dinner: Wednesday-Saturday, 5:30-10 p.m.; Sunday, 4:30-9 p.m.

401 Primrose Road, Burlingame, California
(415) 347-5733

Veal Salinas

3   ounces white loin of veal, lightly floured
2   ounces shallots, minced
3   ounces sherry or Madeira
2   large artichoke hearts, cooked, cleaned, and
    sliced
4   ounces sliced mushrooms
3   ounces heavy cream
2   ounces sweet butter
    salt and freshly ground pepper to taste

Melt butter in a large skillet and add veal and shallots. Cook veal approximately 2 seconds on each side. Remove veal, set aside, and add mushrooms, artichoke hearts, Madeira, and cream. Reduce sauce for about 5 minutes.

   Place veal on top of sauce to warm for a few minutes. Transfer veal to plate and pour sauce over it. Serve with pasta and fresh vegetables. Serves 2.

   Bon appetit!

Fine continental cuisine captures the imagination of the most demanding gourmet at Nathan's Restaurant. Your hosts, Marilyn and Nathan, welcome you to enjoy classic cuisine prepared with skill and imagination. Featuring fresh fish, pasta, chicken, and meat entrées. After dinner, delight in one of our tantalizing desserts or espresso drinks. Also discover our exceptional wine list. Lunch and dinner daily except Monday.

1100 Burlingame Avenue, Burlingame, California
(415) 347-1414

Cracked Wheat Bread

Stage 1

1 cup stone-ground cracked wheat
½ cup water
½ cup honey

Thoroughly combine the above ingredients. Refrigerate for 24 hours.

Stage 2

Combine refrigerated mixture with the following ingredients:

1 cup bread flour
3 cups whole wheat flour
1 tablespoon salt
¼ cup shortening
4 ounces baker's wet yeast
2 cups water

Mix approximately 10 minutes at slow speed. Divide into four equal parts. Hand round. Let stand for 10 minutes. Re-round and place in warm and moist area. Let rise to twice its size. Bake at 400° for approximately 25 minutes. Serves 8.

Le Boulanger (The Baker) is a unique concept in family owned and operated bakeries. Each day we prepare and bake on premises a variety of specialty breads, muffins, and 100% all-butter danishes and croissants from the choicest of recipes handed down from generation to generation.

We feature original San Francisco Sourdough French Bread which received the Grand Prize—Sweepstakes Award—in the Professional Sourdough Competition at the San Francisco Fair and Exposition in 1983, '84, and '85.

Le Boulanger also offers a warm, comfortable environment to stop and enjoy a selection of gourmet sandwiches specially prepared on your choice of oven fresh bread, *seven days a week!*

Hours: Monday-Saturday, 7 a.m.-6 p.m.; Sunday, 8 a.m.-4 p.m. Phone orders accepted.

1420 Burlingame Avenue, Burlingame, California
(415) 579-5843
Also in:
Los Altos—310 Main Street
Los Gatos—133 North Santa Cruz Avenue

Beef Wellington

8 6-ounce tenderloin fillets
8 pieces 4"-square puff pastry dough
1 8-ounce can goose liver pâté with truffles
8 artichoke hearts, fresh or canned
8 large white mushrooms
2 cups basic brown sauce, combined with sliced mushrooms and red wine to taste
3 eggs whites, lightly beaten with 1 ounce water
1 bunch watercress

Sear and brown thoroughly all sides of the tenderloin in a hot sauté pan in a small amount of oil. Place browned fillets in refrigerator to cool.

Spread each sheet of puff pastry with a thin layer of pâté (approximately 1 ounce). Place an artichoke heart in center, then cover with cooled fillet. Wrap dough around meat and lightly seal with the egg white mixture.

Place seal side down in a lightly oiled sheet pan and cover with remaining egg whites. Bake at 375° according to desired doneness: 15 minutes for rare, 20 minutes for medium rare, or 25 minutes for medium.

While Wellingtons bake, prepare mushroom caps: cut off stems and blanch in water with a small amount of white wine or lemon juice to prevent discoloring. Strain and cool.

Prepare basic brown sauce, adding sliced mushrooms and red wine to taste.

Cover a plate with 1 ounce of the brown sauce and place Wellington on plate. Place mushroom cap on top of Wellington and serve remaining sauce on the side.

The Velvet Turtle

Wake-up Smoothie

2 cups orange juice
1 ripe banana, peeled and cut in chunks
2 egg yolks
2 tablespoons honey
1½ tablespoons raw wheat germ

Combine all ingredients in blender and blend at high speed until smooth. (Any fruit of your choice can be substituted for the banana.) Serves 2.

Cappucino

2 cups freshly brewed coffee
2 cups milk
1 tablespoon sugar
1 tablespoon cocoa
1 ounce brandy
1 ounce crème de cacao

Mix all ingredients and bring to a boil. Top off with whipped cream and cinnamon stick. Serves 4.

Cookbook
Committee

After months of tasting and testing all these glorious goodies, there's not much more we can add ... but here are two more recipes we wanted to share—one great way to start your day and one "mahvalous" way to end your evening.

Cole Car Company

Sponsored by Marine Terminals Corporation, 289 Steuart Street, San Francisco, CA

SUCCESSFUL PARTY TIPS

Bruce Krebs Florist
Melinda Brann, Artist
Stuart Rental Company
K & L Liquors
Diet Center

Recipe for a Perfect Party

Choose a theme.
Choose a menu.
Invite your guests.
Call Bruce Krebs Florist.

As most successful hostesses know, a terrific party is composed of good conversation, good food, and great presentation! The "presentation" does not need to be elaborate or expensive, but it should be consistent with the theme of the event.

If you are doing the Hillsborough Luncheon, use a white Italian straw hat as a novel centerpiece. Simply fill a 10″ round waterproof container with oasis, push in a 24″ long lucite or white wooden dowel and attach the hat—gaily decorated with dried or silk flowers, netting, and multicolored ribbon streamers. Fill the container with sprays of fragrant stock, roses, larkspur, lilies, orchids, cosmos, Queen Anne's Lace, and Candy tuft for a spectacular effect.

Place this wonderful arrangement on a full-length pastel tablecloth with a deeply ruffled hem and you've created an elegant centerpiece that will be the hit of the party!

This is just one suggestion—we have many more! Call us with the specifics of your special party and let our creative floral designers go to work for you! We can do everything from intimate dinner parties to elaborate weddings.

Bruce Krebs Florist

We're located in Half Moon Bay and have access to the freshest local flowers as well as exotics from around the world. Our designers are on call to bring a wide variety of these fresh flowers direct to your home for your personal selection. We look forward to creating the perfect flowers for whatever occasion you have in mind!

Hours: Tuesday-Saturday, 10-6; Sunday, 10-5.

302 Main Street, Half Moon Bay, California
(415) 726-1217

The Perfect Party

A caterer is selected and the menu is determined. The florist is contacted to provide beautiful floral and plant decorations. Refreshments are ordered, and a new gown is in the works. Yet, party-planning is only half-completed.

Think about the total environment. Traffic flow—where guests will go when they arrive, and how they will proceed throughout the event. Are there enough tables and chairs to provide adequate comfort? Can the interior decoration of your home be complemented through the use of linen colors, china patterns, and special lighting? Does a patio or deck offer additional space that can be canopied for dancing, dining, or both? Does your back yard or tennis court offer the opportunity for large-scale tenting?

Be aware of all the elements of your party—and don't be afraid to be creative. It takes only a few garden tables with umbrellas, votive lights, and plants to turn an empty space into an intimate and unforgettable setting.

It is helpful (and fun) to sketch a site plan. If guests are seated for a meal, allow ten square feet per person for adequate comfort. If they stand in a reception-type setting, allow eight square feet per person. To this amount of square footage add all other space requirements: buffet, dance floor, staging, bars, immovable objects, and so on. The total square footage of all these elements defines the amount of space that you need.

If you expect a large number of guests—perhaps for a wedding reception—the use of a big tent makes the occasion as memorable as it is meant to be. And if inclement weather threatens, a tent becomes more than whimsical. It provides all the sheltered space you need for dining or dancing—even the ceremony itself.

THE STUART RENTAL COMPANY

Stuart provides outstanding quality and service for modern temporary environments and party furnishings. We offer choices in china, stemware and glassware, silver and stainless tableware, and all accessories to perfectly suit the nature of your event. Eighteen linen colors, sixteen table sizes, and eight types of chairs are available to enrich the party setting. Silver and stainless serving items, from trays to chafing dishes and candelabra, provide the elegant, professional touch. An abundant supply of specialty items for weddings, picnics, and parties of all kinds is maintained in extraordinary condition.

Stuart, purveyor of fine tenting for over 100 years, offers modern tension structures, elegant white big tops, festive striped big tops, and canopies, accommodating groups from eight to 3,000. Our professional event consultants offer on-site surveys, party planning, and information on all aspects of event organization.

The Stuart Rental Company—quality service for special events.

281 El Camino Real, San Carlos, California
(415) 591-4414

Your caterer, florist, and tent and party rental company are the professionals to consult for a memorable party. Their experience and expertise transform your imaginative dreams into vivid reality.

Chocolate Strawberry Cake (Reducing)

2 cups cored and chopped apples
7 eggs
1 tablespoon chocolate extract
2 cups strawberries, fresh or frozen
  (unsweetened)
1 tablespoon vanilla
1 tablespoon strawberry extract (optional)
1 tablespoon Diet Center Lite Sweetener
1 cup Diet Center Protein Powder, chocolate
¼ cup nonfat dry milk
1 cup unprocessed bran
2 teaspoons baking soda

Place first 6 ingredients in food processor or blender and blend well. Pour mixture into a large bowl. Add the remaining ingredients and mix with an electric mixer. Spray a 9″ x 13″ baking or bundt pan with low-calorie, nonstick spray. Pour mixture into pan.

Bake at 350° for 30 minutes. Cool and cut in 8 equal servings. Refrigerate or freeze. (Each 1″ x 1½″ serving equals ⅓ protein and ½ fruit portions and daily bran, milk, and protein powder allowance.)

Avocados with Hot Crab

5 tablespoons butter
⅓ cup sliced button mushrooms
¾ cup chopped celery
1 pound cooked crab meat, diced
¾ cup sliced water chestnuts
3 ripe avocados
½ lemon, pricked over cut side with a fork
1 cup heavy cream
1 tablespoon Dijon mustard
1 teaspoon Worcestershire sauce
½ teaspoon sugar
3 drops Tabasco
1 cup hollandaise sauce
½ cup blanched toasted almonds
1 teaspoon brandy
2 tablespoons chopped parsley
  juice of ½ lime
  salt to taste

In skillet, heat 2 tablespoons butter. Add mushrooms and celery and cook for about 5 minutes, stirring occasionally. Add crab and water chestnuts and continue to cook, stirring, until ingredients are well mixed. Cover and cook over low heat for a few minutes.

Cut avocados in half lengthwise and rub surface with lemon, squeezing slightly to distribute juice. Place in a shallow baking dish in ½″ hot water and bake at 400° for 10 minutes.

While avocados are baking, combine remaining butter, cream, mustard, Worcestershire sauce, sugar, Tabasco, and hollandaise sauce in a saucepan. Heat to almost boiling, stirring constantly. Stir in lime juice and salt. Add the crab mixture and almonds and mix well. Stir in brandy and parsley. Fill avocados with hot crab and top with more almonds. Serves 4.

Melinda Brann, Artist

I paint tablecloths and napkins to order. Most of my work is abstract impressionism.

... for those who wish paintings on their tables as well as their walls.

880 Hillsborough Boulevard, Hillsborough, California
(415) 348-3984

Suggested Wines

California Grill

Menu One: 1983 Frey Zinfandel ($3.99), spicy and zesty, yet not too heavy. Menu Two: Lamb—1982 Crozes Hermitage, Jaboulet ($5.99), smooth yet rich enough to compliment grilled food; Salmon—1984 Kendall Jackson Chardonnay ($6.79), elegant wine with appley nuances, mid- to light-bodied.

Hillsborough Luncheon

Menu One: 1984 Hunter Ashby Chardonnay ($5.50), on the rich side, but excellent with the mousse and soufflé. Menu Two: 1984 Kalinda Chardonnay ($5.99), light and dry, great for shellfish.

Concours Tailgater

Menu One: 1985 Robert Pecota Gamay Beaujolais ($4.99), refreshing wine, clean and fruity; a quaffer. Menu Two: 1984 Boeger Sauvignon Blanc ($5.89), dry, but not too dry, with a delicious aftertaste.

Weekend Brunch

Menu One: 1984 Dry Creek Fume Blanc ($5.99), herbal nose and dry, earthy flavors. Menu Two: 1983 Waldracher Sonnenberg Spatlese, Sherf's Mule ($4.99), fruity, light Riesling with a bare touch of sweetness, delicious and low alcohol.

Moonlight Supper

Menu One: 1983 Chateau Arnauld ($6.99), perfumey, curranty nose and packed with fruit. Menu Two: 1983 Bourgogne Blanc, Bouzereau ($8.50), rich, heady chardonnay, full flavored. Option: 1981 Cote du Rhone, Guigal ($5.79), slightly peppery nose, robust wine packed with fruit.

Please note: All prices are subject to change.

Dinner d'Elegance

Menu One: 1984 Edna Valley Chardonnay ($9.29), somewhat oaky, rich style, great for pasta; 1983 Chateau Beaucastel, Chateauneuf du Pape ($15.99), spicy, peppery aroma, long finish and packed with fruit, great with game. Menu Two: 1984 Bonny Doon Chardonnay ($9.99), vanilla, toasty nose, clean and delicious wine, not too heavy; 1984 Meursault Poruzot, Jobard ($18.95), rich and full flavored, will go great with goose.

Country Club Cocktails

Menu One: 1983 Cuvee Favieley Bourgogne ($5.99), delicious dry white with earthy nose. Menu Two: 1984 Raymond Chardonnay ($5.99), clean wine with touch of oak and smooth finish.

Family Affair

Menus One and Two: 1982 Beaulieu Cabernet, Rutherford ($5.99), oaky nose, soft wine with nice lingering finish. Options: 1984 Christophe Chardonnay ($4.99), light and easy to drink.

Featuring an outstanding selection of premium California and imported wines, offered at prices below retail. Many older vintages are also available. Wine tastings are held in our San Mateo Store.

Hours: Monday-Saturday, 9 a.m.-7 p.m.; Sunday, 10 a.m.-6 p.m.

231 El Camino Real, Millbrae, California
(415) 697-2801
25 43rd Ave., San Mateo, California
(415) 571-7270
3005 El Camino Real, Redwood City, California
(415) 364-8544

Index

Contributors

Kay Allen
Jane Barr
Chris Beaver
Pat Belardi
Susan Benveniste
Barbara Bowen
Meredith Bressie
Carol Bullock
Mary Lou Burr
Gayle Chan
Julie Chao
Tiffany Chu
Sook Chung
Chris Corsetti
Sharon Covington
Vivienne Creer
Carolyn Csongradi

Robin Curtin
Linda Dills
Cessie Dinerman
Claire Drozd
Barbara Duderstadt
Penny Edwards
Sonia Essalat
Pat Feldstein
Georgia Foggy
Linda Foster
Carol M. Garcia
Chris Garrick
Shelley Gilligan
Patricia Green
Eileen Greenberg
Helen Harness
Claire Hein

Colleen Helm
June Hill
Mary Housley
Sandy Kelly
Theresa Kent
Jeanne Klein
Karen Lanterman
Jon Lee
Logue Malouf
Stephany Martinez
Liz McNally
Barbara Mendell
Cindy Montalbano
Ruth Newman
Sandra Papenhause
Kay Perry
Barbara Regan

Buff Rilliet
Ann Schneider
Barbara Shapiro
Joan Sica
Claudia Smay
Susie Spiegelman
Beverly Stowell
Marilyn Sugarman
Athena Troxel
Karen Lila Vultee
Linda Wagner
Andi Wang
Pati Jake Weintraub
Kathy Williams
Carol Wilson
Jeanette Yee
The Cookbook Committee